Secrets of a
Tee Time Girl

Secrets of a Tee Time Girl

**GOLFERS, SCANDALS AND
THE BEVERAGE CART**

Nicole Kallis

CART GIRL PRESS

2004

I dedicate this book to my family,
who loves and supports me no matter what.
You have all of my love.

Contents

Preface

We are going to do this preface bit really short and sweet. If you're like me and tend to skip the preface part, don't. I promise, this is important to the book and really short!

Carol Wayne from the *Tonight Show with Johnny Carson* was the sexy, big-busted, and full-of-fun "movie lady" in a sketch called "Tea Time Movie Reviews with Art Fern." It began in 1971 and continued to be popular for the entire decade.

"What does that have to do with golf?" you're probably asking yourself right about now. Well, like Carol, the beverage cart girl is sweet and quick-witted and can really throw a zinger at you when deserved. Although the cart girl has an obsessive desire to serve cold beverages and snacks, she also has that special desire to greet you and morally support you at most golf courses. But fair warning: she is also watching your behavior and learning daily how to handle men acting like small children. She is jotting her experiences down to memory as though reviewing a movie she's seen earlier that day. I am one of these fine, upstanding young cart girls and I apologize in advance, for I have been spying on you and writing it all down since day — or should I say hole — one.

My goal as your cart goddess: to see you on hopefully

three to four occasions during your four-and-a-half-hour-and-then-some round of golf. Whether you want anything or not, I am always pleased to see people outside, enjoying good health and good times in the fresh air and sunshine. Throughout my day, I hear, see, participate in, and God help me, *instigate* many a story.

Wait for it, here comes the payoff: Well, while Carol Wayne was your "Tea Time Girl," what follows in this book is Nicole Kallis, your "Tee Time Girl," and my "reviews" of the various golf course "skits" I encounter on any given day. So when you see contained within the chapters, "A Tee Time Girl Review," don't be alarmed. It's just me confessing one of my accounts or experiences. You'll meet the Tee Time Girl often.

Enjoy. Don't be offended. Or for that matter, go ahead and *be* offended and hopefully you will see a little of yourself, someone you know, or someone you heard about among the pages to follow.

There, that's it. No more front matter, for you *or* me!

See, I've got your back.

I think you and I are going to get along *just* fine. . . .

Introduction

History from the Cart Girl

It's difficult to say when the game of what we now consider golf was actually first played. Certainly, the world agrees that the location was in the Kingdom of Fife in faraway Scotland. Anyone can read and research that bit of fact and realize there is no argument about it. It's printed in black and white, right there in the history books or, if you do your research online like I do, it's right there on the Internet.

By some accounts, the primitive beginnings date the game itself back to the early 1400s. Of course, back then there was no titanium and none of those cute little Tiger-inspired fuzzy club covers. With nothing but rocks in overgrown fields, back then the game was played with a club resembling a hockey stick and a ball resembling a rock. But even then the attraction of the game was so strong that Parliament had to outlaw the competitions in the 1450s, as they felt their soldiers, who would pretty much be every man alive, were too distracted from their war preparations. Scotland, if you recall from Mel Gibson's famous movie *Braveheart*, was *always* at war.

In 1508, however, King James IV himself took up golf (or whatever it was called in that time) and had to lift the law against the sport for fear of never again being able to win skins at his growing talent in the game. (Skins or furs from animals were used like money is today when gambling. People today still use the term "skins," but now they are made of paper, are greenish in color, and have the face of one of our presidents on it — if the skin comes from America, that is. Fascinating to me is the rainbow of emotion men emit when one has to give one of his skins to another.)

From Scotland, the stick-rock-hole game spread quickly

through Europe. Mary Queen of Scots, of "Mary, Mary, quite contrary" fame, brought the game to France. She actually coined the phrase "caddie" — and this, I think, is really cool — because she used the "cadets" from her army to assist in carrying her sticks and rock around.

How's *that* for abusing your office?

About two hundred years later, the rules of the game, now publicly called "golf," were officially declared and much of the etiquette we abide by even today was formally established. Thus the game was made forever inviting to the fanatical and *almost* neurotic stay-at-home stockbrokers and engineers who most certainly flood your local public course, as they do mine.

In Edinburgh, even before America signed the Declaration of Independence, the game of golf was almost down to a science, right down to the number of holes to be played, needing membership to the club, and having a dining facility and party house for after the game. It is truly incredible to think how little the game has changed since those ancient times!

By the 1800s, golf was quite popular among Yankee men. It was so popular that by the early 1900s, there were over 1,000 golf courses and clubs across the United States. In 1894, The United States Golf Association (USGA) was formed to protect the game in America. They established handicapping systems, and monitored such stimulating aspects of the game as "turf research" (whatever *that* is!).

1900 came along with our very first U.S. Open in golf! Thank goodness they made it an easy anniversary to remember. Hard to believe the U.S. has celebrated over 100 of them. By this time, New York and Massachusetts alone had more than 160 courses combined.

In 1910, a banner year, two items that would revolutionize the sport forever were implemented: the golf ball with dimples for better aerodynamic flight, and the steel-shafted club to replace the wooden shaft, though I think Bobby Jones, winner of the 1930 Grand Slam, used hickory shafts.

Now golf equipment could be quickly reproduced on the assembly line and thus could be made affordable for the average man. (The average golfing woman, alas, was still decades away.) The Professional Golf Association, or PGA, was formed in 1916, the year the first PGA professional championship was played. By 1944 there were 22 events that spread over an entire year. In just the last 60 years, few could have believed that this simple warrior game from Scotland could have grown so big.

Today, the game of golf is like a living spirit. It continually grows, evolves, and changes with the advancements of technology, not to mention the imagination of golf course designers and the fabulous greenskeepers who make their living giving us all beautiful backgrounds upon which to play our favorite sport.

I can't even picture how they used to cut the grass back in fifteenth-century Scotland! Cow mowers, I guess.

Regardless, with history comes tradition, and no tradition is as storied or stiff as that of golf. For those of you who have never actually paid heed to golf etiquette, or who have played the game for years but never quite cared before, here is a list of eight tips to serve as a quick refresher course.

Golf Etiquette

Eight Tips for Those of You Who Need It
to Get Started with This Book

Before becoming a beverage cart girl, I had played golf only several times — and very badly. I am still quite a hack, in fact, but I love the game and, with free golf available to me as an employee, I have improved my skills, as well as my intellectual understanding of the game, considerably over the past few years.

For anyone reading this book that has little knowledge of the sport, this will be like the "blond leading the blind," but the following list should be helpful and can be used as a reference while reading this little book, or playing this big game. The back of the book will also have a glossary to refer to, so if you miss it the first time around, don't sweat: there won't be a test, just reference material.

The following is a short summary of indispensable golf tips that will help to speed up play, foster a love of the game, and share what we in the trade refer to as "that lost art of politeness." It will also help to distinguish you as a golfer; one who has not only a high regard for the game, but also for its history. Your confidence will also improve because you will no longer have other players constantly correcting your behavior on — and off — the course. Golfers are notorious for letting you know the minute you cross the line when it comes to etiquette, but if you try to follow the below-mentioned tips, they will see that you at least know how to behave yourself on the course and no one will be shouting, "Off with his head!" (as may have been the case with Queen Mary and her "cadets"). You could call these the Homeric rules of golf (rules handed down from generation to generation, orally, that is until someone wrote them down. . . . I think). And if they've never been written before, though I suspect they have, somewhere, here they are for the first time:

1. Moving, making noises, or standing too close to a player who is about to hit their ball is known as "teeing off the tee off," and is definitely not a great way to form a lasting friendship with the rest of your foursome!

2. Wait until the group in front of you is far enough out of your way before hitting so that even on your best impact with the ball, there is no chance for it to roll, bounce, or (God forbid) land in their playing space. This is also for safety reasons: a golf ball can kill if you hit someone on the head with it. A corollary to this rule would be that, if you *do* see your golf ball flying toward the inevitability of contact with a human body part, do the owner of said body part the courtesy of yelling "Fore!" be*fore* it does so. They may not listen to you — it's a little like the boy who cried wolf if you do it enough times — but at least you will have made the effort and will score points.

3. Always play what I like to call "ready golf." This means that if you are ready to hit and other people in your group need more time to set up, then don't delay. Hit your ball. Also, don't delay leaving the putting green. Once you "hole out," leave the putting green immediately. (Holing out is when everyone

has finished putting and you put the flag back into the hole.)

4. Invite faster groups to play through, unless, of course, the whole course is playing slowly, such as on a busy weekend or crowded holiday. Be forewarned: Etiquette should not equal "getting taken advantage of." After all, if you let *everyone* play through, you could be looking at a nine-hour game.

5. Clean up after yourself. Repair all divots and ball marks on the tee box and the putting green, rake all footprints in sand traps, and add sand to all pitch marks on greens and fairways. Pitch marks are bits or chunks, as the case may be, of earth that are scraped up by your club when you swing to hit your ball. Some call this a chili dip, turf burger or other

names that we won't get into here but will discuss later in the book. A divot or pitch mark should look like a slice of bacon, not like a pork chop.

6. Don't step on the line of another player's putt. The line, in case you were wondering, is from the player's ball to the hole. To avoid this most egregious of golfer faux pas, just walk around. Remember, this is supposed to be a game played for your health, not just for your convenience. The extra few steps could actually be good for you.

7. Don't drop clubs on the putting surface, even though everyone *else* does. (I believe over on the edge of the green and the surrounding area of grass is acceptable, however. I think they call this area the apron.)

8. Carefully replace the flagstick in the hole after everyone is finished putting out or, as above, holing out. If you're wondering whether or not this is your responsibility every time, just because you now know some golf etiquette, rest assured that this is usually the job of the second-to-last person to finish putting, as the other two golfers are supposed to advance to the next hole. Don't worry, it's a speed thing.

That's it! Do these few things properly, even though in actuality there are probably a whole lot more, and you will find yourself making lots of new friends on the course. And here's a ninth tip, on the house: never stop learning.

When you see a new piece of golf etiquette, something shown to you by an older, more experienced golfer, a cart girl such as myself, a golf course employee, a friend, a family member, or even just a newbie, fresh to the game and thus more "book smart" than the rest of us combined, file it away and keep it handy.

Chapter One

The Pro Shop

It may not be important to you, but the pro shop is where I start my day! My experience in the pro shop is not at all limited. Before moving over to the snack world, I worked for a small stint receiving golfers, making tee times and ringing in purchases at our course pro shop.

In my capacity as a pro shop worker, there was not a whole lot those golfers could do to spoil my day. For minimum wage, after all, it was not worth it to let anyone ruffle my feathers when they, in turn, got to spend the whole day golfing. Occasionally, I will still cover for someone in the pro shop when they need to use the restroom and it's actually fun to pick up the phone and book a tee time or check in a golfer, just for old time's sake. A great schmooze tip, if you want to test out your buttering-up skills, is to get really friendly with the person checking you in and, when you think you've got them on your hook, ask if they are allowed to give friends and family an employee guest rate (usually 50 percent off). Then ask if they'd be willing to extend that rate to you. Hey, it's worth a try, right? You can pay me back later for that one! If they do it, give the dog a bone. It doesn't obligate you, but since they saved you a bunch of money, share the wealth.

As a rule, I've noticed that women seem to spend far more time in the pro shop than men. The guys can't get out of there fast enough. They want to pay, get a scorecard and a pencil, and find a sign to tell them where the bathroom is.

Occasionally they will look for socks if they forgot to wear them, golf shoes if they forgot to bring them, buy some Texas Tees (these would be super long tees, for those of you not familiar with the Lone Star state, although they sell them everywhere), and they might even be tempted to buy the new 500-series driver.

In my opinion, of course, the 300 series is big enough, but then I prefer a smaller head size. The need for more head on a club is definitely "a man thing." Once the customer has paid, be it a man or a woman, there will be no time wasted inside when there is a starter calling their name.

Ah, be it ever so agonizing, the ever-hopeful day of playing a perfect round of golf lies stretched out and beautifully manicured before you!

Rule of Thumb in the Pro Shop

Get In, Pay, Get Out.
End of Story . . .

Oh, yeah. I almost forgot: During this brief moment of paying and checking in, many a golfer, young, old, male and female, can be heard crying softly to themselves, but loudly enough for at least four others to hear, about the following. They cry about:

- The green fees (golf prices)

- The heat

- The cold

- The rain

- The tee time availability

- The price of balls

- The tournaments (walk-on golfers without reservations especially!)

- The lady golfers

- How slow the computer is

- The seniors (and if it's a senior, then the women)

About that time, I like to say something subtle like, "Excuse me, sir, would you like a couple of my Midol?"

Nah, not really. Most of the time I let them know that I will be their beverage cart girl and I ask them what, if anything, they would like me to put on my cart to allow them the best possible time on the course. I also let them know that if they persist in whining, crying, or sobbing, I do, in fact, carry tranquilizers, ropes, and Nyquil.

Chapter Two

The Marshals

On a golf course, a marshal is an official of ceremonies, in our case the ceremony being golf, festooned as it historically is with rituals galore. They take their charge with great pride and conviction. Most of the marshals at our course are retired gentlemen. They are nice as can be to me, except when losing money (skins) to each other golfing, and on or off the course these men are never too busy to throw me a smile.

"What did they do before becoming marshals?" you might be asking yourselves. (Or maybe not. Do you always talk aloud when you read like this?) Their careers before retirement range from airline pilots, CEOs, bankers, doctors, and politicians to former school janitors. If you're thinking marshals are just paper tigers, however, rest assured: they are the cops out there and, if they feel it is appropriate and necessary for the safety of the other golfers, they'll throw you off the course. (Or, in the case of our marshals, it's more like "threaten to throw you off." I have never seen anyone dismissed from a round by a marshal at our course, or any course, for that matter.)

I am sure you all know this already, but I didn't, so I'm saying it on behalf of those readers who are new to golf: these marshals don't work for much pay. What they work for is access to free golf. If it's not too busy, you won't see much of them. "So where are they?" Well, if you must know, they're out looting the bushes for recently devoured golf balls. (Yes, I swear, there are such things as ball-eating bushes. Although I haven't exactly seen one in action, many a frustrated golfer has told me stories, usually as he buys a pack of back-up balls from my cart. So I know they're real, just like Bigfoot and the Loch Ness Monster.)

Being some of the first employees to the course, as the marshals are each day, certainly entitles those of them who so desire to hunt for the pick of the golf ball litter that is birthed and abandoned every day on the course. Great balls — and even the occasional piece of equipment, such as ball markers, club covers, or even abandoned putters — are very important to possess for an addicted golfer, and I can definitely attest that anyone who works for free golf is certifiably addicted. Club covers and putters can be found in the lost and found at the pro shop. Don't bother asking if anyone found your balls. They will just look at you funny.

Addicted or not, most of these guys work weekdays and weekends and really don't need the job. But that doesn't make them dummies. Who *wouldn't* want to be outside in a golf course setting during their "golden" years? (Although, for these guys, a new term might be their "green" years.) There are beautiful big trees, freshly cut grass, flowers, free sodas, and great people to say hello to every day.

From free golf to free balls, courtesy of the ball-eating bushes, that is, it takes a lot to get under a marshal's collar. Take, for example, "Andy." A former CEO of a *Fortune* 500 company, Andy has gobs of money. He can afford to buy golf balls for himself and everyone else on the course, for that matter. If he wanted to, he could fly wherever he wanted and play golf all over the world. But he's come to a point in his life where he just wants to stay in the neighborhood. He's definitely not bored at the course. After all, a lot of his friends work there, and, most importantly, he not only wants to find all the lost golf balls, but he actually *needs to* in order to feel complete. (It's an addiction, kind of like playing FreeCell on the Internet for you young ones who know what that is.)

Besides, I think Andy is also at a time in his life where he believes the Golf Ball Bunny comes out every morning to hide the balls while he is out loading the course water coolers, and if he doesn't go on his own private hunt, the other golf marshal "children" will find all the good golf ball eggs.

After a long, hot Sunday, moving an unruly troop of golfers around the course at a ridiculously slow pace of play, Andy can sometimes be heard chuckling as he unloads his basket of balls. The funny thing is, he turns right around and gives the balls away to the cart girls, the administration staff, the maintenance crew, and even some of the nicer members of the club. He's kind of like the Robin Hood of golf; taking from the rich (or, in this case, ball-eating bushes, trees and the occasional weed patch) and giving to the poor (in this case, municipal golf course employees).

As a matter of fact, he gives them to everyone *except* the crew in the pro shop. I am pretty sure that's because they recently changed the sign on his cart from "MARSHAL," which sounds impressive, to "COURSE AMBASSADOR," which is obviously a little too diplomatic for his taste. As a matter of fact, Andy doesn't like to be called an Ambassador at all. It's as if the golf gods took all the bite out of his title.

Marshals could kick you off the course. Ambassadors? What can they do? Negotiate a treaty to ask you to be escorted off the course in a fair and timely manner according to basic UN rules of diplomacy?

Where's the fun in *that*?!

I hear sob stories all the time from golfers who have been scolded by a marshal. (Don't eyeball your golf shoes, you know who you are.) These downgraded golfers cry that their five-some had to be broken into a three and two. (Poor babies.) They whimper that they were told to "speed up" or to "clean up their act." (And, most times, rightfully so.) They whine,

"He yelled at me for playing a second ball." (Of all the nerve.)

Well, Zippy, there are rules you must follow in order to play a second ball and by your actually admitting to it being your so-called "second ball," you're probably playing a third or fourth, if the truth be known. I know this because I often get stuck waiting for you guys to tee off and I've seen as many as *six* balls played. Not by a foursome, a five-some, or whatever you'd call a six-some, but by *one guy*! I'm really not sure what stroke number you're up to by that point, what, an 18?! So, Mr. Cheater, save some tees to go with your whine and put the ball back in your pocket. Okay, I am off the subject. (Get used to it!)

Let's get back to the marshals "picking on you," shall we? Look, not everyone wants to play a six-hour round of golf and if the marshal doesn't keep the course moving, then we end up closing the course as the sun is coming up the next day. Hey, there's an idea: 24-hour golf courses. I can see it now: klieg lights and miner's caps and those light-up neon shoes like the kids wear. Hmmm, maybe not.

Twenty-four-hour golfing or not, sometimes the marshal is right, fairly playing by the rules just helps make golfing safe for all. Other times, the marshal is clearly wrong, falsely accusing you as the course's slow play culprit du jour. Hey, somebody's got to do it, but until the Golf Channel brings instant replay to the public links, just nod, smile, and stop quarrelling with 70-year-old men.

Despite popular opinion, the marshals aren't trying to be nattering nabobs of nascent negativity. I'll have you know the majority of them took the job because it was supposed to be "stress free." Isn't that what golf's all about, after all? So try to make life easy for them. (If you don't want to consider it your civic duty, consider it a humanitarian effort!) Agree to speed up your game or clean up your act, or whatever, with them (even if you don't agree), and then do what you want the minute they are gone.

Trust me, they're not going to hang around or stalk you to make sure you're complying. They just want to feel important, validated, and — most importantly — *justified*. In other words, they don't want to feel like paper tigers. So do them a favor and do what they tell you! They have driven all over the course all afternoon and, whether you believe it or not, know more about what the pace of play should be than you or I possibly could. I work with them, so I know, and for that reason I will usually defend them.

There is nothing worse for golfers than a backed up course. Two foursomes on every hole, waiting on every shot, a stacked tee box, eight golfers waiting for the wannabe pros on the dance floor (i.e. putting green) to finish an eight-handed game of croquette. Oh, the horror! To boot, they're all doing their "Plumb Bob" dance around the flag hole.

PLUMB BOB — A method of aligning a putt or reading a green. Believe it or not, construction workers started this deal as they use a tool called a "plumb" to align target points. On a golf course, you do this by facing the hole and raising the putter shaft to eye level (using your *dominant eye* only!), aligning the bottom of the shaft or putter head on the ball. The amount of distance left, or right, of the cup hole is the approximate break left or right of the putt. A friend explained this bizarre ritual that golfers perform before putting when I asked, innocently enough, or so I thought, "Why do all the golfers stand around with their putters raised up in front of them?" It makes sense now. I'm not sure it helps the golfers *make* the putt, but at least now I get it.

So tell me now: what is worse, an occasional comment from our sweet old marshals, or the above said mind-blistering and baffling behavior on a busy Labor Day weekend when you still have to make three trips to the liquor store and a grill to fire up when you get home?

Hell, mind-blistering? That's my signal! There is nothing better for the beverage cart girl than the above list of pains-taking maneuvers golfers use to try to get their ball in the hole. I am here to ease the suffering of the afflicted golfer by pouring him or her a drink, offering a smile, a sly comment like, "Hey gorgeous, how's your day going?" and I can serve and make happier many a golfer who is stuck with nothing better to do than drink and "Eat My Cart Out!" Oh, darn. I got off the chapter subject. (Surprised yet?)

Well, to soften the blow, here is the first of those "Tee Time Girl Reviews" I promised you in my intro. (If you didn't read it, go back now. I'll wait.) You'll recognize the setting, and I'm sure you'll see yourself, or at least someone you know, in the cast of characters throughout my book.

And now, here she is, your very own Tee Time Girl to tell you all about it! (Applause)

The Tee Time Girl Review

DAY: Tuesday
TITLE: Morning Has Broken
SET-UP: Eight marshals playing golf

Marshals usually have one day a week when they all meet first thing in the morning (and I mean morning with a capital "M"!) and golf together. Most of them are good old friends from back in the day. Now, I've never actually played a full round — or even a full hole — with the marshals. When I first started, I felt terrible that these magnificent guys were given the tee times that no rational, practical, sound person ever wanted. In time, however, I learned never to link common sense to golf. Apparently, a freakish love for early morning comes with age. There appears to be great gratification taken in the tradition of being "first off." But first off before sun-up? Ouch! Count me out.

Perhaps that's because these guys are usually retirement age, sleep about three minutes a night, and play the first three holes in that funky time of morning when everything is gray. Not dark, not sun-up. Gray. Their definition of the word "determination" finds new meaning and their perception of determination isn't qualified so much by their result, as by their pace of play. Good golly, but they play the course fast!

By the time I arrive at the course for my morning preparations on the cart, these guys are already energetically driving up the eighteenth fairway. Why is it that older people seem to live in an accelerated time zone? They want to get up at 4:30 a.m., tee off at 5:00, finish by 7:30, and yet eat lunch at 9:00 a.m. (I can't tell you how many times they have come in and asked if the hot dogs were ready) and then drive miraculously slow on the highway home for their nap. Then they wake up to live another full day before bedtime? Two days in one. Like burning the candle at both ends, I guess. I thought only teenagers did that.

In the rare instance that I *have* been on the course as early as when the marshals are out there, I always make it a point to jump off the cart and hit one off the tee box with them. (The tee box is where a golfer tees his ball up on that oversized tooth pick and hits the ball for the first time on that hole.)

When I get a-hold of the ball, I can really send it out there! They like to call this "crushing" the ball. Usually, I hit it something terrible, though! I mean, I'm fresh off the cart and haven't hit or practiced at all and they are already on their 12th hole as the sun comes up.

To their credit, these gentlemanly marshals are always really supportive when I "mess up" and give me lots and lots of advice. On the day in question, a marshal we'll call "Bono" let me hit with his "special club." Its enormous club head (designed by NASA, no doubt) reflected the morning's sunlight in its ultra-light titanium molding. As he handed it to me, I proceeded to tee it high and slaughtered the ball. That's one of the things with older men — they can smile and make a cute flirtatious comment even after you outdrive them by 30 yards. (Try that with the young ones, they run off pouting and stop buying things from your cart for a week as "punishment"!) I'll say this much, after watching that ball sail off to a fond adieu I sure hope Bono leaves that club to me in his will!

This temptation to abandon my cart girl duties for a moment to grip and rip doesn't only occur with the marshals. Sometimes on a slow day I will jump off the cart with regular golfers to hit one. When I see my regulars on the course, I don't even have to ask anymore; they just hand me a club, a ball and a tee.

My best "marshal's sketch" occurred when all eight of them were on the 18th tee box. I asked if I could "try to hit one." A new marshal named Mac, much younger than the other fellows — by that I mean in his early 80s — handed me his club, he said, "You can use mine if it's not too big for you."

Now, this old bird knew exactly what he had said and, I

could tell, was hoping to get some sort of mild reaction from his innuendo. Not knowing me as well as the others, of course, he could not have prepared for my response. Hey, I'm not shy. Subtle nuance, I don't even know what that means.

Here's the dialogue for our little sketch that ensued:

Me:

(*Mock coyly*)

TOO BIG FOR ME, EH? I'M NOT SURE IF THAT IS SOMETHING YOU CAN EVER SAY TO A WOMAN! BUT I'M AFRAID BONO HAS GOT THE ONLY STICK I WANT TO SWING.

The Marshals (except for Mac):

(*Giggling like school girls*)

TEE, HEE, HEE, HEE.

(I have no shame and Bono has already put what will someday hopefully be my club — that famous club that I hit further than any other club ever, but still belongs to him for the time being — into my hand. Wow, there was some good psychobabble!)

Me:

SEE, I REALLY ENJOY THE WHOOSHING SOUND A GRAPHITE SHAFT MAKES.

(*I grasp the club.*)

PERSONALLY, I AM A CONTROL FREAK AND SO I USE THE "VARDON"/OVERLAPPING GRIP. IT WAS NAMED AFTER GOLFER HARRY VARDON. IN IT, THE PINKY FINGER OF THE BOTTOM HAND OVERLAPS BETWEEN THE INDEX AND MIDDLE FINGER OF THE UPPER HAND. I'D FEEL JUST

TERRIBLE IF MY HANDS SLIPPED OFF THE END
OF THE SHAFT.

(*I wink at Mac.*)

I MAY NOT BE ABLE TO MAKE THE BALL TRAVEL
TOO FAR, BUT AT LEAST I'LL STILL HAVE THE
STICK IN MY HANDS.

(*Said with innuendo galore.*)

The Marshals:

(*Now giggling like naughty high school boys*)

TEE, HEE, HEE, HEE.

Mac says nothing and is about the same color as the ladies'
tee box markers. So I teed up my ball and crushed it! (Thank
goodness, I'd have been really embarrassed after talking all
that silliness, and then duffing it.) Returning to my cart, I
handed Bono his club and told him it was "perfect."

Me:

(*To Mac*)

THAT WAS REALLY GOOD FOR ME . . . WAS IT
GOOD FOR YOU, TOO?

Mac and I joke around all the time now.
  I love this job! And I love this game!
  As you will shortly see. . . .

Chapter Three

Etiquette and Manners and Style – Oh My!

More like lions and tigers and bears — and sometimes, unidentified animals. I'll break this chapter down just as it is, in order: etiquette, manners, and then style — oh my!

As we have briefly touched on up to this point, the rules and etiquette of golf are plenty. Those who play with any amount of awareness know at least the basics:

1. Be quiet when one tees off;

2. Let the person furthest from everything, the green, or the hole, etc. hit first (the ever-playful "you're still away" line I hear so much when I participate), and;

3. Most important, never ever step on someone's line. (This means, do not walk in front of a person's ball line to the hole.) Some people will come up to the line and take one giant step over it (or nearly over it), and others will leap like a ballerina, while still others make only a small, effortless step over the line. Others will pass behind the golfer and ball, while still a few more will travel all the way around the flag from the other side. What is up with any of that? It takes time, and it all looks silly. I mean, good manners aside, I say, when it's your turn to hit, get to your ball, line it up, plumb bob if necessary, and hit your ball. But this is golf and it is an extra polite game until, that is, someone has a super big temper tantrum.

Greenside Etiquette

The player furthest from the hole is to hit first. Once everyone reaches the dance floor (green), all players are to mark their balls, lay their clubs gingerly around the apron (the grass just off the green, cut very short but not as short as the putting surface) of the green, and stand off the green until the person furthest from the hole putts. What could be simpler than that, I ask you?

As we all know, putting can be a really tedious process when the rules are followed to the letter! Especially when you get golfers who seriously believe there are hidden cameras around the course and that their game is being televised! Ashton Kutcher, look out! (He is a really cute famous actor for those of you who don't recognize the name.)

These guys line up their ball to the hole, squinting through one eye, then get up and go all the way around to the other side and do the same thing. Then they squat down, stand up, practice stroke next to the ball, squat down again and, finally, they putt the ball.

After all that foreplay, however, they invariably miss the hole; putt the ball, miss, and then three-jack the putt for a six on a par three! What a nuisance! I blame television. These guys watch way too many PGA champions and attempt to copy their actions down to a "tee." But you know what? If I thought it would make me a better player and I wasn't afraid that someone would scold me for taking too long, I'd try all that stuff too. Quick, somebody tune the violin and give me some sympathy here. One of my all-time favorite lines to say is when a golfer putts the ball and the ball circles the lip of the hole but doesn't drop in. "Ooo," I say. "Prom

Night." When they ask me what that is, I tell them, "All lip and no hole."

Here's another one: (The girl needs theme music, by golly.)

The Tee Time Girl Review

DAY: My day off to golf with the boys
TITLE: To Duck or Not to Duck???
SET-UP: Four, no, eight, no, twelve
waiting on the tee box

There is one move that I, without a doubt, love for the utter over-the-top technique golfers use to perform it. Golfers sometimes pick up a little tuft of grass and throw it up in the air to determine how their ball will be affected by — get this — the wind, if struck properly. I think that unless you are playing in Hawaii or someplace else notorious for serious wind, say, Antarctica, your ball is just not going to be that affected by it and you're better off playing the ball straight without all the grass pulling and time wasting.

The foursome I was accompanying on one of my days off was on the tee watching the exceptionally slow group ahead on the fairway hit a variety of "dogs" and "Fatty Arbuckles." (See the glossary to follow, I don't want to spoil the suspense!) They worked their way to their third shots only 100 yards from the tee box on this long five-par. Clearly, they were not playing a "scramble," which from the look of it might not have helped this group anyway. Three of the players had hit and the fourth was taking more time than Steve Ballesteros on a *very* bad day. (Ballesteros was fined at the 2003 Italian

Open and refused to accept a penalty stroke for taking too long. Funny thing is, he said he was being picked on by the tour "mafia".) By this time another foursome has gathered up on our tee and four more are fast on approach. After carefully lining up his shot, he actually picked up some of the grass and tossed it in the air on this hot, sunny, windless day.

Far from giving him wind speed and any other useful climactic variables, however, his large hunk of long grass quickly returned into his face — and open mouth. To the now 12 people on the tee box waiting to hit, we were howling and laughing and crying so hard I thought we would all need swimwear by the time we were through. We were all ready to wet ourselves silly. I mean, we had no idea we were going to be surprised with a show *and* golf that day. Who can tell, maybe this guy was a remarkable wind player and was having a rotten golf day due to its lack thereof. (Speaking of which, a tail wind could have really helped this guy, too.)

Perhaps if it *had* been a windy day, he wouldn't have shanked his ball out of bounds and into the yard of a neighboring home. A "shank" is a shot struck on the part of the club head where the heel is joined to the shaft. It makes the ball travel dead right, assuming you are right-handed. The shank is typically considered the worst shot in golf. It is even worse than a "whiff," and that's when you swing and miss the ball altogether. The ball in question went zooming over the heads of two gardeners on the patio. With textbook comedic timing, as the ball shot off the clubface, one of the twelve shouted loudly, "quatro." As the ball bulleted by within inches over one gardener's head, he ducked, while grabbing his amigo, a much smaller man (like comparing a Doberman and a Chihuahua), and pulled him toward him. When the ball smashed into and shattered the glass door, the big gardener now lay on top of the little guy and shielded his body with his own. Maybe you had to see the whole thing to really get the visual, but I hope I am doing the story some degree of justice.

So the bad golfing story goes on. After providing the proper identification to the gardeners to give to the homeowners, the golfers did eventually reach the green. Seemingly unaware of both life's and nature's lessons, he again tossed some grass in an attempt to verify that, yes, there was still no wind! This time, however, it was on the putting green. The putting green! I can understand why he took so long on *that* putt. By our count, he needed it for a "15," a number you can't even put on a scorecard. A marshal showed up and we all applauded. They were three holes behind and they were instructed to pick up their balls and move up. We didn't see them for the rest of the day, not even in the 19th hole, better known as the bar.

Guess it was too "windy" for him in there. . . .

The Tee Time Girl Review

DAY: Sometime last year
TITLE: Tossed Salad
SET-UP: Four golfers

On this day, I was on the beverage cart, watching and waiting for this group to putt out. Well, this one guy in the foursome was a real yapper. I mean, you couldn't shut this guy up. He's all, "Should we take the pin out or leave it in? They say there is a 76 percent ratio (ratio, he said ratio) that the ball will go in if you leave the pin in — okay, we'll, leave it in. . . ."

Finally, a moment of silence as one of the other golfers putts his ball and narrowly misses the hole.

Immediately, the Yapper sets off again, "Ohhh, too bad. Okay, me next, same thing, leave the pin in, I was watching the Golf Channel and they said, blah blah blah . . ." Well, the ball hits the hole, smacks into the pin, and bounces off the stick, and comes to rest some three and a half feet from the hole.

The Yapper starts screaming, "Why didn't you pull the pin, it was going right for the hole?" and on and on. This guy went beyond on and on and on. Now, you know the poor guy tending the pin would have been dammed if he did or didn't. Pull the flag, that is. On my next go around the course, this guy was still crying some four holes later! Doing it loudly, all the while his playing partners were trying to hit.

Etiquette, manners, and wooohhh! If his manners weren't bad enough, you should have seen what this guy was wearing! If you took the professional golfers Duffy Waldorf (sick daisy print shirt, pants, socks, and I've heard even his underwear), Jasper Parnevik, tight checked body suits (checkers and checkmate), David Duval, lately referred to as Buffy the fashion slayer, known for his fondness (total obsession) for dark clothing, and Faldo (can you say bright, pink and LOUD?), and tossed them in a salad bowl with a mayonnaise and chocolate dressing, you'd have the Yapper's dress faux pas. The fairway was his personal beauty pageant catwalk for the Mr. Golf Universe contest!

For the most part, I've observed that golfers look pretty darn spiffy. The requirements on most courses are: Collared shirts, soft spikes and *no denim*! Rules for women are pretty loose, too: no hot pants, no denim, and no spaghetti-strap tank tops.

The majority of golfers look great, and I pay attention to that kind of thing, so I should know, but every now and then you get a goof ball out there and I actually have to avoid eye contact to keep from laughing. I mean, you actually experience the awkwardness that they themselves cannot for some reason feel. The worst so far was a very wealthy woman in her mid-40s or 50s wearing tons of make-up and jewelry, and wearing a hot pink, plaid mini-skirt with matching top and jacket, a plaid barrette, and white knee socks. Yes, I said knee socks. (Yes, I also said *white* knee socks!) Yikes! (Don't get me wrong, I'll bet she was something . . . before electricity! By the way, I *loved* Rodney Dangerfield in *Caddyshack*. I loved Chevy and Billy too. It's one of my all time favorite movies.)

Chapter Four

18 Jokes from the Dud Golf Ball Collection

Golfers are famous — or should I say *infamous* — for their humor. (Or lack thereof, and, if you spend as much time on a golf course as I do, you know exactly what I mean.) Here, then, is the best — or should I say worst — collection of golf jokes I've collected over the years. Enjoy!

Joke # 1

One day a man was out playing golf, when he sliced his shot off into a patch of buttercups. Rather disgusted with himself, he went in search of his ball. After finding it, he was ready to hit the ball back onto the fairway when he heard a voice say, "Please don't hurt my buttercups."

Startled, he looked around to find the source of the voice, but to no avail. Again, the man prepared to hit his golf ball and once more he heard the voice say, "Please, don't hurt my buttercups." This time when the man looked to find the source of the voice, he saw a small leprechaun standing by him. The little man spoke to the man and said, "Please, sir, if you will kindly pick up your ball and throw it up onto the fairway instead of hitting it with your club, I will reward you with a year's supply of butter for free." The man thought about the offer for a minute, then replied, "That's a fine offer, I have but one question for you: Where were you last week when I hit my ball into the pussy willows?"

Joke # 2

A man is stranded on a desert island, alone for ten solid years. One day, he sees a speck in the horizon. He thinks to himself,

"It's not a ship." The speck gets a little closer and he thinks, "It's not a boat." The speck gets even closer and he thinks, "It's not a raft." Then, out of the surf comes this gorgeous blonde woman, wearing a wet suit and scuba gear. She comes up to the guy and says, "How long has it been since you've had a cigarette?"

"Ten years!" he says.

She reaches over and unzips a waterproof pocket on her left sleeve and pulls out a pack of fresh cigarettes. He takes one, lights it, takes a long drag, and says, "Man, oh man! Is that good."

Then she asks, "How long has it been since you've had a drink of whiskey?"

He replies, "Ten years!"

She reaches over, unzips the waterproof pocket on her right sleeve, pulls out a flask, and gives it to him.

He takes a long swig and says, "Wow, that's fantastic!"

Then she starts unzipping the long zipper that runs down the front of her wet suit and she says to him, "And how long has it been since you've had some *real* fun?"

And the man replies, "Wow! Don't tell me that you've got golf clubs in there!"

Joke # 3

Four guys who worked together always golfed as a group at 7:00 a.m. on Sunday. Unfortunately, one of them got transferred out of town and they were talking about trying to fill out the foursome. A woman standing near the tee said, "Hey, I like to golf, can I join the group?" They were hesitant, but said she could come along once "to try it" and they would "see what they thought."

They all agreed and she said, "Good, I'll be there at 6:30 or 6:45." She showed up right at 6:30, and wound up setting a course record with a 7-under-par round.

The guys went nuts and everyone in the clubhouse congratulated her. Meanwhile, she was fun and pleasant the entire round. The guys happily invited her back the next week and she said, "Sure, I'll be here at 6:30 or 6:45."

Again, she showed up at 6:30 Sunday morning. Only this time, she played left-handed, and matched her 7-under-par score of the previous week. By now the guys were totally amazed, and they asked her to join the group for keeps. They had a beer after their round, and one of the guys asked her, "How do you decide if you're going to golf right-handed or left-handed?"

She said, "That's easy. Before I leave for the golf course, I pull the covers off my husband, who sleeps in the nude. If his member is pointing to the right, I golf right-handed; if it's pointed to the left, I golf left-handed."

One of the guys asked, "What if it's pointed straight up?"

She said, "Then I'll be here at 6:45."

Joke # 4

Golfer: "I'd move heaven and earth to break 100 on this course."

Caddie: "Try heaven, you've already moved most of the earth."

Joke # 5

When I start out on the first tee, I feel like Tiger Woods. But after nine holes I feel more like Winnie the Pooh.

Joke # 6

A little girl was at her first golf lesson when she asked an interesting question:

"Is the word spelled p-u-t or p-u-t-t?" she asked the instructor.

"P-u-t-t is correct," he replied, before elaborating: "*Put* means to place a thing where you want it. P-u-t-t means merely a vain attempt to do the same thing."

Joke # 7

A young man who was an avid golfer found himself with a few hours to spare one afternoon. He figured if he hurried and played very fast, he could get in nine holes before he had to head home. Just as he was about to tee off an old gentleman shuffled onto the tee and asked if he could accompany the young man, as he was golfing alone. Not being able to say no, he allowed the old gent to join him.

To his surprise, the old man played fairly quickly. He didn't hit the ball far, but plodded along consistently and didn't waste much time. Finally, they reached the ninth fairway and the young man found himself with a tough shot. There was a large pine tree directly between his ball and the green.

After several minutes of debating how to hit the shot, the old man finally said, "You know, when I was your age I'd hit the ball right over that tree."

With that challenge placed before him, the youngster swung hard, hit the ball up, right smack into the top of the tree trunk and it thudded back on the ground not a foot from where it had originally sat.

The old man offered one more comment, "Of course, when I was your age that pine tree was only three feet tall."

Joke # 8

A foursome is waiting at the men's tee when another foursome of ladies are hitting from the ladies' tee. The ladies are taking their time and when finally the last one is ready to hit the ball she hacks it about ten feet, goes over to it, hacks it another ten feet, and looks up at the men waiting and says apologetically, "I guess all those f***ing lessons I took this winter didn't help."

One of the men immediately replies, "No, you see, that's your problem. You should have been taking golf lessons instead."

Joke # 9

A couple of women were playing golf one sunny Saturday morning. The first of the twosome teed off and watched in horror as her ball headed directly toward a foursome of men playing the next hole. Indeed, the ball hit one of the men, and he immediately clasped his hands together at his crotch, fell to the ground, and proceeded to roll around in apparent agony. The woman rushed down to the man and immediately began to apologize. "Please allow me to help. I'm a physical therapist and I know I could relieve your pain if you'd allow me," she told him earnestly.

"Ummph, oooh, nooo, I'll be all right . . . I'll be fine in a few minutes," he replied breathlessly as he remained in the fetal position, still clasping his hands together at his crotch.

But she persisted, and he finally allowed her to help him. She gently took his hands away and laid them to the side, she loosened his pants, and she put her hands inside. She began to massage him. She then asked him: "How does that feel?"

To which he replied: "It feels great, but my thumb still hurts like hell."

Joke # 10

It was a Sunday morning and four good buddies were at the first tee. Number one said, "This golf game is costing me dinner for my wife tonight."

Number two said, "That's nothing, I had to agree to my wife's parents spending the weekend with us."

"Ha!" said number three, "I had to give my old lady the credit card to go shopping."

Number four said, "Boy, are you guys ever screwed up. I woke up this morning and the wife asked what I was planning. I replied, 'Golf course or intercourse?' She said, 'Take a sweater' and went back to sleep."

Joke # 11

Question: Why do golfers always carry two pairs of trousers with them?

Answer: Just in case they have a hole in one.

Joke # 12

Question: Where can you find 100 doctors all at the same place on any given day?

Answer: A golf course!

Joke # 13

Two golfers are sitting at the 19th hole discussing their games this year when one says to the other, "My game is so bad this year I had to have my ball retriever regripped!"

Joke # 14

Question: What's the difference between a bad golfer and a bad skydiver?

Answer: A bad golfer goes: "WHACK! Damn!" A bad skydiver goes: "Damn! WHACK!"

Joke # 15

Question: Did you hear about the Mexican golfer who got shot yesterday?
Answer: Yes, they said it was a hole in Juan.

Joke # 16

The only difference between driving in golf and driving a car is that when you drive a car you don't *want* to hit anything.

Joke # 17

Two longtime golfers were standing overlooking the river. One golfer looked to the other and said, "Look at those idiots fishing in the rain."

Joke # 18

(For the 19th hole. Where all
the stories are told, anyway.)

A golfer has one advantage over a fisherman: He doesn't have to produce anything to prove his story.

Chapter Five

Signals: You Guys Are Killing Me!

All in all, I've learned a lot from my time behind the wheel of the snack cart. My advice to those who want to avail themselves of my various services: don't be shy. The golf course is not a library. Etiquette or no, there's nothing between you and a good signal to grab my attention. This is not the Masters, either, so you're more than allowed to use your voice. I know that I have said you're supposed to be quiet when someone is teeing off, putting, or just hitting the ball, but in between, you are always welcome to use your voice to communicate. You do when you get mad at yourself, anyway, so why not use the same bravado — or should I say vibrato — to get *my* attention?

Far from being a nuisance, it's always great to be stopped on the course. It's what I live for as a beverage cart girl. Well, that's not entirely true. Much like strippers, tips are *really* what I live for! But tips or no tips, I am in the service business, and I truly strive to meet the golfers' needs. My goal is to check in on each golfer every four holes during your game. I can't always do it and everyone should know why. Golf etiquette extends to the cart girl as well and a lack of it is prevalent on the course these days.

What is the reason for Cart Girl Etiquette? It's simply the laws of supply and demand. When I get stuck waiting on each hole for golfers who don't want anything, yet insist I wait for everyone to tee off or putt out before they "decide," then I am lucky if I can see you twice in your entire round, let alone my usual four times, so if I seem like I am in a hurry to go through, it is only because I want to service those in need of me — or my products. However, there seems to be some confusion out there. It begins when you want me to stop for you and when you don't.

First, be perceptive of the fact that while I am a reasonably clever woman, I am *not* telepathic. (Lucky for you!) What I am trying to say is that as I am approaching your group, I will be looking for some kind of unrestrained gesture. Subtlety is not necessary. Please also try to understand that my cart is so noisy, I can barely hear what *I* am saying let alone hear my cell phone ring. I am sure if you were able to see yourself zealously waving, while shaking your head from side to side, you would understand the confusion.

Here's what works for me:

How to Say "No"

1. Use your voice *and* your hands. Say something like, "Not this time, but check back on your next round" while waving your hand in a "No, No" type of way. This gets your message across — "No, not yet" — and yet at the same time makes me feel hopeful: "Maybe next time."

2. Say, "No, thank you!" and smile.

3. Say, "We're good," and give the famous "thumbs up" gesture. (The Snack Cart Girl hates the word "No.")

How to Say "Yes"

1. Wave frantically and jump up and down.

2. Give us a forefinger up — a "Wait a minute" gesture, if you will.

3. Light up your eyes and drive toward us really fast with your mouth open wide. If you have a passenger, he or she may feel free to wave their arms or a club for emphasis.

4. Say, "Am I happy to see you," "You are a vision of exquisiteness," or any manner of other nice things.

The Ones that Positively *Don't* Work

(and Absolutely Kill Me)

1. Ignoring me. I am required to ask everyone on the course if they would like something, and am not trying to bug you. I don't work on commission, so it's not in my best interest to be overly aggressive. In other words, I'm just trying to help.

2. A thumbs up all by itself. What does that mean? Are you good? Are you bad? Does that mean, "Yes, you want me?" "Your round is going well?" "What?" (This is a very iffy signal, so try to be more specific.)

3. When one person answers for him/herself without checking with his/her fellow players. They give me the old, "I think we're good" line. Yet the other members of your "some" could be starving, dying of thirst, in need of spare tees, or all of the above. Golfing is not a solitary sport: Ask the other members of your group before you answer for them and wave me on by.

4. Behaving in an irritated way, mumbling to yourself and making weird hand gestures as if we can't see you. (Frankly, it alarms us!) From then on, we won't stop even if you even if you burst into flames.

Hey, it's time for Tee Time Girl. I think, by now, she really deserves to have some theme music.

The Tee Time Girl Review

DAY: A Friday
TITLE: A Bad Boy
SET-UP: A twosome on the fairway

Okay, so I'm driving along and two golfers are on the fairway. I slow down and one of the guys start waving his hand in front of his face like he just passed a little lethal gas. Sue me, I take it for a "go on by" gesture. So then he yells, "Wait a minute!" He makes a straining face and then starts walking toward me, waving his hand again. Man, I hope it wasn't one of those kinds that stick to you. I'd hate for him to bring his stinky wind bubble all the way over to me. (By the way, I thought the farting scene in *Blazing Saddles* was funny, but the lactose-intolerance farting scenes in the Wayans movie, *White Chicks*, had me rolling!)

Anyway, he gets over to me and starts looking in all my compartments and he's asking me for everything I *don't* have. Then his friend comes over. Now, his friend is really young and cute. His friend starts looking in all my compartments, too. Farty man decides he doesn't want anything but the cute guy decides on a candy bar, a sandwich, a beer, and some of my red vines that I told him were special things that I brought from home to give to my big tippers. He didn't tip me, and I think his farty friend stole a few things from the cart. My count wasn't right at the end of my shift. I should have ignored the "wait a minute" comment and just kept on going. After all, the snack bar was only one more hole away.

Chapter Six

Psychobabble, or: Did I Actually Say That Out Loud?

Psychobabble: This is defined as the internal voice that amuses us, points out our insecurity to us, and on the golf course, can be your worst enemy. It's the voice that, after an errant golf shot, says, "What the f✳✳✳ did I just do?" or "Why can't I hit the ball like I do in my practice swing?"

For me, I get my psychobabble the worst when I have to deal with really cute, confident guys my own age. Luckily, most of them are working or in school and can't afford to golf every day, or even every week, so my internal ravings don't surface *too* terribly often.

What I'm thinking when Ms. Psychobabble rears her ugly head: "He is cute. Oh, dear God, he's going to ruin this moment by talking. Hey buddy, are you trying to make eye contact? No, no, those aren't my eyes, those are my breasts."

Unless I am feeling particularly witty or sassy, I try very hard to keep my mouth shut. (For obvious reasons!) Inside, though, I am thinking, "Should I ask if I can hit a ball? No, that's not a good idea, Nicole. Remember the last time when you completely embarrassed yourself? Nicole, you're married with kids, stop it. But, hey, it doesn't matter where you get your appetite, as long as you eat at home, right? Oh man, what am I thinking?"

Trust me, there are enough rambling thoughts to fill the rest of this book, another entire book, another entire trilogy, for that matter. (J. R. R. Tolkien, look out!) Come on, guys. I'm a girl, remember? Cuckoo, cuckoo!

On keeping my mouth shut, I discovered a long time ago the key to appearing oblivious: I try to take on the mindset of a man. I am aware of only "me" and feelings that apply to me, or, for that matter, to what I want.

When it comes to guys that are out of my "able to accept them as a potential mate" age range (and, as far as I am concerned, that would be 50 and older), my psychobabble is much less severe.

Usually this guy has his career set. If he's married with kids at home, then he's put on an extra 30 pounds of lovin'. And if he hasn't, his wife has! If he's single, divorced, married, has kids, doesn't have kids, it doesn't matter. They're all sort of thinking alike.

These guys are thinking they need adventure and excitement and if they can fulfill it on the golf course, then so much the better. I have many a man in this age group with a crush on if not me then at least one of the other cart girls I work with. These guys are relatively harmless and definitely the most fun to joke around with. Hands down, they are the most creative, confident, and most interested in me on the golf course. I tell you, if I were a woman in need of a good man, I could come to this course on any given day and pick out a good 30 or so of them! They are also the best tippers, most certainly! For that I give them a deep and well-intended "THANK YOU!"

You guys are buried in life, kids, survival, making money, and trying to "have a little fun." Please let me know if there is anything I can do to make your day a little brighter on the course. You are, without a doubt, a welcomed presence.

Chapter Seven

The Unbearable Lightness of Seniors

"The only reason I play golf is to bug my wife.
She thinks I'm having fun."

—ANONYMOUS GOLFER

Assuming that light is a metaphor for goodness and truth, then darkness is where the evil dwells. Well, speaking of the Dark Lords of the Golf Course, here then goes my (very) candid opinion on seniors.

In a nutshell, "there ain't much time left." So leave 'em alone and let them have a little fun, or misery, or crankiness, or harmless flirtatious fun. Be patient and kind to them and give them whatever the hell they want. (Blunt enough, eh?)

They can be a little sensitive, sure, but most of them have been around the block a time or two; that means they will try to get away with all that they can. Seniors live to play and be played with, and the men *love* to flirt.

My favorite line I like to throw out to them when I come up on their tee box is, "Hi ya, gorgeous. Do you feel as good as you look today?" This always gets a positive and flirtatious comeback and gets them closer to my mobile cookie jar. When they get close to the cookie, as we all know, it's hard for them to resist. So my advice to you other young ladies out there is to instigate the flirting. It makes their day. The senior women watch their senior men like hawks, because these women *know* their men. They know that the older their husbands get, the younger they behave. It's just not on the golf course, either. But you guys already know that, don't you? Heaven love you, you old bastards know just about *everything!*

Before I know it, they've got their wallets out and they are throwing money at me for no reason at all. Then I leave and they wonder what just happened. Now, that's not entirely fair. (Or entirely accurate, for that matter.) Actually, these guys are getting a fixed income for the most part and their company — Social Security, Inc., you may have heard of it — doesn't pay very well, so to say they are the best tippers in the world is pretty far off the mark. But you've got to give them a break. They all know the value of a quarter, and don't think for a second that they are not trying to dupe you into believing that they don't have a clue about its current buying power. Again, seniors will try to get away with anything. Most of them will wave me on and don't want to be bothered. I wave and I smile.

However, I have found the senior loophole. My uncle Dan, who had golfed all his life, had his own definition of the word G.O.L.F.: Getting Old and Living Fine! They all love free stuff and thus my experience of the big senior group day on the course begins. . . .

Can you hear the music? Yes, it's her again to review the experience . . . Tee Time Girl!

The Tee Time Girl Review

DAY: One of the weekdays. That's
when they get the senior rate.
TITLE: A Bushel of Seniors
SET-UP: Men (mostly)

I'm thinking to myself as I am loading the cart for the day, *How am I going to grab their attention?* It doesn't just come naturally, you know. I actually have to *invent* ways to make better tips. One that works (almost) every time is to pay very close attention and flirt shamelessly to one unassuming senior per foursome. Why just one? It drives the other three crazy! And I do lots of special things for this guy, like give him a cup of ice without him asking for it, or dig deep into my cooler for the coldest soda for him.

At that point they will start competing, and that's when they reluctantly dig out their senior "bank roll." The dusty wad of dollar bills emerges into the bright morning sun. As an aging, spotted hand reluctantly pulls an extra dollar off, you can actually see George Washington squint, his eyes sadly unaccustomed to the light.

I know I'll be making change today, quarters, dimes, nickels, pennies, and some other fluff from their pockets thrown in for good measure. I don't need to load the cart with a bunch of stuff, but I'll take some golf balls and hope they're willing to let me hit a few and be playful. But what can I give them to get their attention? I start digging around in my purse and, ah ha! Victoria's Secret chocolate mints! They'll love them. Now I've got a reason to create more dialogue lines: "They're not just for panties anymore!" Or: "Victoria's Secrets, something else to put between your lips besides panties." (Lots of blushes on this one.)

Anyway: Most of them let me hit a ball and didn't mind that I could outdrive them with a cold, a flu, and a hangover

combined. Some actually got a little something else from my cart than just the mints. I actually went home with some paper tip money that day! Cute, really, I couldn't wait to see them on my next round and, hopefully, they couldn't wait to see me, either!

Chapter Eight

Lady Golfers

Female golfers are very serious. When women learn how to play a game, they tend to go a little overboard about learning the etiquette and the rules. When they play with each other, furthermore, it is extremely competitive. I would say even *more* competitive than men are when they're playing seriously. As a matter of fact, women are far too serious for the kind of golf they play. It's not the LPGA out here. Still, over-serious or not, women usually keep to themselves and drink water from home. For the most part, I just wave as I go by and smile. It is said amongst the trained professional roving mixologists, "You'll make no hay on Ladies Day." No need to stop here, at least for the food and drink sales. Ice is another thing though. With so many having hot flashes these days, women have been known to tip a dollar just for offering ice on a sweltering day, but for most women, the idea of tipping is akin to speaking a foreign language. Women by and large simply do not tip . . . that is, unless you happen to be a young, cute, male Greek Adonis type. That's when the billfolds whip out like fireworks on the 4th of July and the conversation leans toward who is the Adonis more willing to escort? Mother or daughter (prom or ball)?

To the untrained eye, female golfers seem harmless and sweet. Their large sun hats and bright clothes make them easy to spot. Most men would believe that if left unchecked they could clog the flow of a golf course like the arteries of an obese man living on an all-bacon diet. Actually, this is just really not true, at least not the women at *my* course. At my course, the women rock! They are usually the ones nipping at the heels of the foursome of guys in front of them! The majority of women on almost all golf courses are from my mother and grandmother's generation. They were brought up in the '40s and '50s and even the Depression era. Most women married as virgins and their men took care of them financially so the women could stay home to raise the children. And hence they now belong to the ladies club at their country club. They are a powerful and respectable generation of women. Most of them have had to struggle their whole lives to prove that they were as capable, if not more capable, than men. Unfortunately, and I am not exactly sure where women get it from, but they can be the most critical, insecure people on earth, and not just at the golf course. It's such a contradiction: Women need to support each other more, yet unstead, we can be so catty with each other. Yep, I too can be caught on the wrong path to the sweetness of one's heart. One comment about my serving POWERade instead of the other stuff can send me into a temper challenge like nothing else. I am a big fan of the NHRA and NASCAR and POWERade is my choice, too. Come on, race fans, there's nothing like getting *fully blown*.

They act like they hate themselves, and nothing is ever good enough. They hate their weight, their hair, and their nails. They don't think they keep their house clean enough, and they criticize their golf swing mercilessly. (Almost as much as they criticize their children, husbands, maids, siblings, neighbors, etc.) I think it's a real shame because their idea of fun is really warped. And ladies, I am also guilty as charged.

Fortunately on my course, our ladies group is relatively small and I love them all. I know many of their names, and they know me, too. There are 14 regular Wednesday players and there can be as many as 32. Yep, it's true, "you'll make no hay on Ladies Day," but at my course, I don't care. I am there to provide a service and it is their option to use it or not. I am glad to see them out there. Better yet, I am proud to see them doing something for themselves and taking care of themselves.

I am sure most cart girls at other courses feel the same way about *their* women's group. I know I am one of the lucky ones because I've played at other courses and boy, oh boy, the tales you will read! Since that day, I refuse to play on Ladies Day. On this particular course, they had not 14, not 32, but 50 regular ladies. I'm so lucky; I picked a day when there were 75. I think 75 women golfers each week would make me quit my job.

Now then, if you are the type of person who will slam this book shut due to hostility, then you must skip the rest of this chapter. I am not nice in the experience I share. Fact is, this next section is a major bitch-fest. The men from my test group who have read it cry laughing. The women who read it think I need therapy — and hate me. Again, I love women, I respect women, and all women are my sisters. Okay, that sounded a little freaky. If you read on, just remember: This is all meant to be humorous.

Really.

I swear. . . .

The Tee Time Girl Review

DAY: Monday
TITLE: A Bad Apple
SET-UP: 75 lady golfers at a different course,
before I became a cart girl

Before I became a cart girl, I lived north of San Diego. I unexpectedly had a day off and decided to see if the nearby course had room for a single walk-on. They said I could join the threesome on the tee box or I would have to wait a few hours before they had an opening. Do you think they could have sugarcoated that for me? I really knew nothing about golf at the time, but I loved it and tried to play any chance I could. They asked the group if I could join them, and they said it would be okay.

I was to be riding with Bunny. Yes, I did say Bunny. I bid farewell to the pro shop and eagerly loaded my clubs into Bunny's cart. I was taught the value of manners and social skills at an early age, and was ready to use them. I was about to introduce myself, thank Bunny for her kind offer to let me ride with her, and extend a firm handshake to my newfound "friends." But at that exact moment Bunny began to waggle her rather wrinkled finger back and forth, in an attempt to lay down the "Laws According to Bunny." Now, I must mention that, despite my upbringing, that finger waggling crap never worked for my mom, and Bunny will receive no more recognition of it than she. I hate finger wagglers!

Bunny:

NOW THEN, I AM A SERIOUS GOLFER. I HAVE
TWO RULES AND, IF YOU FOLLOW THEM, THEN
I'M SURE WE'LL GET ALONG JUST FINE. YOU WILL
NOT TAKE THE 'LORD'S' NAME IN VAIN, AND
YOU *WILL NOT CUSS.*

Wait a minute, I thought to myself (and let me underscore this moment because I remember it so vividly). Did I have "speak to me like a child" written on my forehead? To say that Bunny and I were not to become fast friends would be the embodiment of the word "understatement."

I quickly realized that I was about to embark on a mind-numbing trip to the thirteenth ring of hell, with a walking yeast infection as my personal tour guide. My skin crawled as I forced a smile back to the now gray and ashen-faced Bunny. But, lo and behold, Heaven was there to help me as the course goddess came motoring up. She was about to pass us by as I have learned to do on Ladies Day, but she caught the desperate glimmer from my eye and probably noted that I was not from the same planet as my riding partner. She stopped. Thank God! Bunny never said anything about not drinking. I asked the cart girl to wait for just a moment so that I could properly address Bunny.

Me:

(*Extending my hand to hers,
teeth only slightly clenched*)

IT'S A PLEASURE TO MEET YOU, BUNNY. MY
NAME IS NICOLE. YOU KNOW WHAT? I HAVE AN

EIGHT-YEAR-OLD DAUGHTER WHO I GOLF WITH,
SO I'LL JUST PRETEND I AM TALKING WITH HER.
BUT NO SITTING ON MY LAP WHEN WE DRIVE,
OKAY?

Not surprisingly, Bunny didn't get the sarcasm. Then again, she might have gotten it and just ignored it so as not to encourage me any further. For the love of God, it's me saying stuff out of proportion to stress a point, and I poured that gravy on pretty thick. I mean, sh*t, Jiminy Cricket already. Sure, a few of the men are pigs (and other species to be covered later), but at least around *them* I can be an adult with the freedom to be myself, right?

It was obvious that Bunny would have none of that. That's okay, the cart girl was waiting for me. Beer never tasted so good that day.

Not surprisingly, all of the ladies teed off before me. Not surprisingly, they were all very nice, easy, safe tee shots. Surprisingly, as I rarely feel the next emotion, *I* was a little nervous, but I was there for a good time, so I teed off, and I'll be damned if that ball, bless its dimpled little heart, didn't go farther and straighter than ever before!

"YES!" I heard myself say rather loudly. The other ladies, seeing that maybe they had a hopeful new player to join their group, now all approached and shook my hand and introduced themselves to me. *Lovely ladies,* I thought. *Why couldn't I ride with one of them?*

I was one of the gals now, and Bunny wasn't going to intimidate me into behaving like a sheltered, disciplined child. I got into the cart and said loudly enough for her to hear, but still under my breath, "F***in' A!" as I cracked open my beer. This was the only swear word I used for the entire day and

I was respectful not to take her "Lord's" name in vain. My Lord really doesn't mind. I just had to rebel the one time. Okay, the second time.

We were both very quiet for the remainder of the round, which incidentally may have scarred me for life. The good news is that if I were ever to be abducted by terrorists, or alien creatures from another planet, my tolerance to torture has been immeasurably improved.

I pride myself in seeing the best in everyone, so I did manage to find something positive and pleasurable in the experience: She was a dreadful golfer and I took pleasure in *that*. Actually, she would have to be coached just to get *up* to being called "dreadful." She also had enlightened the term "serious golfer" to also include "dismal human being." She was so critical of everything. She reminded me of women who constantly think they look fat. I can't stand that. And I can't understand how this woman could take something as great as golf and transform it into . . . into . . . well, definitely *not* golf, though I am not sure what to call what she *did* turn it into. But what really gets me is how someone can be so miserable that they feel compelled to come back and do it every single week, making it miserable for everybody else in the process. "Nurse! Where are you when I need another beer?"

I have to admit that I played quite well for those 18 holes, despite having a really boring time save seeing the cart girl. Bunny would sear a hole into the grass with her eyes every time I shouted out, "YES" from a good drive or putt. I abided closely enough to "Bunny's Rules," however, so that I was kind of missing that joyous feeling I normally feel when I get to take a day off to treat myself to four-and-a-half hours, or in this case six-and-a-half hours, of pure, unadulterated golf.

To this day I shiver even to recount the experience. By the

end of the round, the lead lady told me I could golf with them again anytime and that I should join the ladies group there. I don't know. I think for once I'll follow the "Once bitten, twice shy" rule.

At all costs, I will only golf with the women I know at my *own* course. They let me be myself. Little kisses to you all and thank you for keeping it small and friendly.

Chapter Nine

Ten *Don't Ever Do*'s with the Cart Girl!

1. Don't expose yourself to us. It's nothing we haven't seen before and, frankly, we'd rather see your wallet crack open than your zipper. (For more rumination on this "don't ever do," please see the chapter "Freaks, Geeks and Cock-a-Roaches,")

2. Don't stiff us on our tip. We work hard, day after day, in the hot sun to make your lives better. You wouldn't stiff the bartender at the 19th Hole, now would you? So why would you stiff us?

3. Don't yell at us. We're cute and nice and we're here to serve you. You're big, loud, and scary. No one will be on your side if you do.

4. Don't block us in. Be aware, at all times on pathways, around tees, and greens, to park as far to the side as possible.

5. Don't get us drunk. (You won't get any special favors; you will just get a louder, slower, sloppier cart girl who won't be able to drive very well and will doubly curse you the following morning when she's hungover, Louie.)

6. Don't crash your cart into our cart. It may seem like a funny idea at the time, but don't do it, you big bad doggie! Remember, there are a lot of lawyers who play golf and when your smaller, lower golf cart is stuck under the rear of my bigger, higher beverage cart, it will be pretty easy to figure out who was at fault. (And how much it's worth!)

7. Don't ask us to race. Our cart has a motor on it and, frankly, we'll kick your ass. Then, while we are celebrating our victory, you'll get mad, complain, and then I'll be the one to get into trouble. It's your classic lose-lose situation.

8. Don't get excited. (You know what I mean and it grosses us out.)

9. Don't ask us to have sex with you or to go on your fishing trips with you to Cabo. We're not whores. If we were, we wouldn't be doing this, and you probably couldn't afford us anyway.

10. Don't have a temper tantrum in front of us. We may laugh at you, or you might scare us and we won't stop again on our next round when you really need us.

Chapter Ten

Ten *Always Do*'s with the Cart Girl

(TRUST ME, SHE'LL LOVE YOU FOR IT)

1. Give her a dollar just for being out there.

2. Let her pass by if you don't want anything before you start to putt out or tee off. Her cart is pretty speedy and it won't take long to get away.

3. Tell her she's your favorite cart girl. (You might end up with better service and you'll probably make her day.)

4. If she really *is* your favorite, offer to pay off all her credit cards!

5. Offer to let her hit a ball!

6. Offer to let her play the whole hole with you. She'll refuse most likely as it would probably be too much time off the cart, but it's a nice offer.

7. Believe me, we really want for you to have some quiet time when you're putting, so wait for us to get out of harm's way from the guys hitting up behind us, and let us stop the cart for you. (However, if you're just starting to putt, please refer to #2. If your carts are blocking her, somebody, come and help her move the carts off to the side and then buy something just for the hell of it.)

8. Buy something. (It doesn't get any simpler than that!)

9. Give her five dollars just for being out there! (Come on, she's worth it!)

10. Enjoy yourself. It's golf, folks, not a trip to the doctor!

Chapter Eleven

Tournaments:
The Royal Treatment

Tournaments, I love 'em! Imagine, if you will, a wide-open field of freshly cut grass filled with rabbits, gophers and mice. You are a puppy and all your kitty and puppy friends are about to be freed from the pound for a day of play. This, my friends, is what human beings call a golf tournament. At check in, there is coffee, Danish galore, orange juice and a Bloody Mary bar. After golf there is always a party with food, prizes, booze, and a lot of laughter. And during the tournament, there is golf and your favorite beverage cart girl! (Sometimes I think you'd rather play with the cart girl than play golf. I'm right, aren't I? Come on, you can tell me. 'Fess up!)

Quite often these tournaments are both fun *and* business. Sometimes the golfers get tickets that are good for most if not everything on the cart, except me, of course. Now, while a gratuity *is* attached at the end of the tournament, it is split up between 11 people, leaving me with about $10.00 and that, my friends, just isn't fair for the kind of service I provide. I dutifully explain in a most charming fashion to them (as slowly as possible), making it quite clear that "the tip is not included in that little ticket!" This works surprisingly well! It's all about being clear and never assuming that people have mind-reading abilities. People will do what you tell them, but you've got to spell it out, even at home.

Other tournaments are really lavish, with different booths on every hole. From winning a new Harley-Davidson, to massage chair therapists, to margarita stands, the sky is the limit. It's a social event, often a day out of the office and, as such, very upbeat. Seldom does anyone ever play serious golf in this kind of setting, unless they're absolutely, 100 percent clueless, and it's really a blast out there. Everyone is drinking, and because it's co-workers and friends, it's totally out-of-control drinking. I love out-of-control, but I care if you're driving and I always ask.

Quite often the post-tournament is followed immediately by a banquet with another bar, prizes and never enough food. Occasionally a group of my new boyfriends invite me to join them. Most of the time I can't, as I end up working at those, too, as a server or bartender. Lately since our head chef quit, I have been barbecuing at them too. Surprise!

A fanfare can be heard in the distance as the Tee Time Girl is seen riding up on her white golf cart. . . .

The Tee Time Girl Review

DAY: A nice hot Saturday in the summer
TITLE: A tournament and a guy named Louie
SET-UP: A pull-out-all-the-stops tournament!

Tournaments are the best when they are big! The tournament in question for this Tee Time Girl Review had 220 players. They took over our whole course. They had a gourmet coffee bar on the first hole, muffins and pastries on the second hole, margaritas being blended on the fourth hole, a massage therapist on the sixth hole, contests to win a car on the eighth hole, sausage and sauerkraut being barbecued on the turn, a motorcycle to be won on the 11th hole, a trip to Hawaii on the 14th hole, and, on the 18th hole, a chance to win $100,000.

I was thinking to myself, *What the hell do they need a beverage cart for?* This is where I learned that sometimes it is just seeing a familiar, friendly face a few times that can make all the difference to a golfer's game. Also, many of the guests wanted beer and Bloody Marys. (I have to admit, I make an amazing Bloody Mary. And you thought I was humble. Shame on you!)

On my course, I carry a full bar on the cart with me. On top of that, my margarita is rather authentic, wink, wink, nudge, nudge, so more guests were getting mine than those overrated frozen kiddie drinks from hole four. The day was great.

There are always one or two groups in a tournament that always stick out. On this day, it was Louie's group. They were loving my Bloody Marys and they came on a day when I brought my own spicy pickled green beans to sub for the pimento olives. It started getting wild when they wanted to continue with vodka, but also do shots of tequila. Yummy. Louie had two shots plus a Bloody every time he saw me. He saw me five times before his group was ready to go to the dinner/awards ceremony. You do the math. The man was plowed and in love and jumped into my cart hoping I could take him on a joy ride. I slyly asked him for his car keys and without knowing what he was doing; he gave them to me. Talk about obeying my every command. Then he did a double take. It was a deer in the headlights moment and he started begging me to give the keys back. It's incredible how quickly he seemed to sober up. I told him my dilemma. See, as a bartender of sorts and being the person responsible for how messed up he was, I would be held partly accountable in the event of a terrible accident in which a death were to occur. He seemed to understand and he called one of his buddies over. What he did next was such a turn-on. He told one of his buddies that he was too drunk to drive home and could he get a ride with him. It brings tears to my eyes when sweet stubborn drunks make the right decision. I gave his buddy the keys and we all hugged and parted ways.

There were lots of hugs and smiles and prizes and, I must admit, I made more in tips that day then I ever had before. Although the golfers were competitive for the prizes, they were having the best time just getting out and playing in such a festive and loose atmosphere. It makes my job so great when I see people having a terrific time. A famous quote from my dad comes to mind: "You weren't put here on earth to have a terrible life or a bad time." It really puts things into perspective for me. I use that line all the time. This is your life.

Have some fun with it!

Better yet: Pretend every round of golf is a tournament. (Now *there's* a thought!)

Chapter Twelve

21 Words the Male Golfer Cannot Turn into Something Sexual

(BELIEVE IT OR NOT!)

1.

2.

3.

4.

5.

6.

7.

8.

9.

10.

11.

12.

13.

14.

15.

16.

17.

18.

19.

20.

21.

Chapter Thirteen

You Cheat and I Know It!

(ON YOUR GAME, ON YOUR JOB,
ON YOUR WIFE!)

If a tree falls in the woods — and no one is around to hear it — does it make a sound?

A friend once told me he was a compulsive liar: he lied to everyone all the time and would, at some point during our friendship, lie to me, too. (He wasn't lying about that one, boy! I mean, he lied every chance he could get.) I told him that most people lie and lie very well — but you really can't lie to yourself. You may do a bang-up job convincing yourself that the lie is the truth and you may not even be clear on your own reality, but you know inside when you're lying. Does it hurt anyone? In life, integrity is important. I think the vast majority of people strive to achieve a high level of personal integrity.

However, it seems to me that you cannot always get a complete picture of a person on the golf course. On the golf course, does lying hurt anyone? No, I don't think so. I mean, how far can your lies go on a golf course? So, you lie about how many strokes you took and that your ball didn't land in the woods, and yes, your ball really *did* land on the fairway. Hell, if no one's looking, kick your ball closer to the hole before anyone gets up to the green. I've seen it done. If there's money on the game, it's a little harder as you're being watched, but it happens all the time!

Cheating on your job. Well, what can I say? You're not at work, now are you?

Cheating on your girlfriend or wife? As we all know, golf is the ultimate player's zone. Men come on to me all the time. Married men, devoted fathers, singles with girlfriends, they come in all shapes and sizes. Doesn't matter to them: Hit on me they will.

Frankly, I get more business cards and scribbled-down phone numbers on torn-off corners from their scorecards than I know what to do with. I think it's funny, really, but I feel sorry for the wives and girlfriends sitting back home thinking their man is just out playing a harmless round of golf. (Worse yet, the men really *do* think it's harmless. But that's another entire book in itself.)

I mean, the women pining away back home are not there to hear the tree fall — but he is — and the sucky thing is, he simply doesn't care. But that's Hollywood, folks! It's also politics, religion, and — let's get real — reality. Game on if the light is green, and you can't know if it's red or green unless you ask.

What can I say? You love this beautiful girl. Dum, Da, Da, Dee, the Tee Time Girl!

The Tee Time Girl Review

DAY: A weekday in October
TITLE: Liar, liar, pants on fire!
SET-UP: Not at my home course (mistake)

I was introduced to a golfer by one of the marshals. The marshal knew I had a business venture in mind, and this particular man, not naming names, had developed a business that had made him multiple millions. The marshal thought maybe he could help or advise me, but asked that I "be discreet" and not mention that I knew of what he did. Naturally, my approach was really slow. (It would have been anyway, I'm no fool, but I didn't tell my marshal friend that. Remember, those guys — like all guys — like to think they're teaching you something.)

We exchanged e-mails and he never sent anything personal, just really funny and perverted golf jokes. I loved it. Sick, twisted humor, no problem for me, and if it's golf, even better. Besides, it was mass mailing, not *personal*. After about a month, I asked if he might be willing to advise me and possibly have a look at my business plan and that I knew of his business success because I had Googled him. He then said we could "golf and talk." (Well, like I said, golf is pretty harmless and it's easy to stay conspicuous.) Great, I love golf and he said we could talk. Perfect!

I think not. What chapter are we in again? Oh yeah: Cheaters! *Extremely wealthy* people — and I am talking that top three percent who normal everyday people never get to meet — are often naughty, bored people who are constantly trying to invent new, unique, and harmful ways to entertain themselves. After the first hole, it was pretty clear to me that I was not going to be talking about my business plan anytime soon (read: ever!). I didn't end the game right then and there. Why? Well, seeing as I'd never played the

course, it was a nice one, I thought at least I'd have that going for me. And, frankly, I figured I could handle this guy.

The game took a strange — but not entirely unexpected — twist when he wet-lipped the following words out: "Every hole you win, you get whatever you want. *Anything.*" So I ask, "Even cars, clothes, trips, jewelry, real estate, and on and on?" He nods, "Yes," but check this out, the guy then continues by saying that every hole *he* wins, he gets to give me, wait for it, "an orgasm."

First off, how dumb does this guy think I am, and second, gross, with a capital "G." I don't know about you, but what made this guy think that a young, in-shape, pretty and clearly married girl, would get so turned on by money that she'd allow a shriveled-up, old, married man even so much as kiss her beyond what her grandpa does? No! No! No! No! No! There are too many young, hard, sexy fish in the sea if I were headed down that particular road.

I think, at that moment, he even made me throw up a little. Okay, I can bullsh*t with the best of them, and the day was clearly about bullsh*t. Was I disappointed? Yes! Was he a liar and a cheat? Yes! Did I ever speak to or receive e-mail from him again? Ewwww! God, no! I banned him from my e-mail recipients list the minute I got home that day. I feel really sorry for his wife because, clearly, there are enough gold-diggity women who fall prey to this kind of sick, twisted greed. I'm sorry, but I don't need money like that. Did I hear the tree fall in the woods? Sure did, but you can bet your sweet ass that his wife didn't. There is always something to learn, no matter how strange the lesson, so I played a few holes before I just had to get out of there. This was the first time I ever had to quit a game of golf.

I do miss the e-mail jokes, though!

Chapter Fourteen

Cart Girl Slave

(AT YOUR SERVICE)

Tee Time Girl, at your service. No set up, just the review. . . .

So it's the end of my shift and Lauren, the second cart girl, was taking over the rest of the course. (Lauren, by the way, is the model in all of the photos you've seen in the book. Yep, she really is a cart girl, among other brilliant things.) I am at the 15th hole and ready to say goodbye to one of my favorite foursomes from the day when they "proposition me."

One of the guys says, "So, how much will it cost to buy you as our private cart girl for the rest of the day." They added in, "No funny stuff, just serve us drinks and keep us company." So I set my price. After all, this was an experience I could not refuse. I told them they could "buy me" and anything on the cart for $200.00. Within seconds the guy had his wallet out and two bills were in my face.

Oh boy, here we go. My cart from my quick calculation only had about $100.00 worth of merchandise left on it and the guys had carte blanche to everything. They modestly started with beer. At the tee box they insisted I hit a ball and play the entire hole with them. Yippie. This is the coolest job ever! Not only that, but I parred the hole. The guys were knocked out and I was feeling like if someone didn't tie my swelling head down with ropes to some of the giant boulders, that I might fly away.

Time for more beer and a shot of whiskey for everyone. I was going to have a headache that night. I was instructed to take a shot, too. What, the slave girl should refuse her masters? I think not, and besides, I had already had one of the girls clock me out from the snack bar, so, quite officially, I was "off duty."

After the shot, my "masters" commanded that I go to the

12th hole and, whoever was there, I was to offer them whatever they wanted. Okay by me. I was their cart slave so off I went. These guys and a girl on 12 were thrilled. Free beer. How random is that? I mean, nobody just sends the cart to you to take whatever you want. They offered to tip me, but I refused. I told them I was "already bought and paid for."

When I got back, my masters asked for the scoop and asked if they tipped me. I told them the foursome was delighted and that they offered to tip me, but that I refused. Out came another hundred-dollar bill for me. (Wow, see how that reverse psychology really pays off?!) I felt like such a good little slave!

We all played the next hole and at the tee box of 18, we had to wait for the foursome in front of us, who in turn was waiting on the foursome in front of *them*. The guys offered the gentlemen anything they wanted, too. Pretty soon, the foursome behind us and one of the marshals approached. Bloody Mary's for all, except the marshal and me, that is. By the time we finished the round, the guys drank and ate the entire $100.00 worth of stuff and I was walking away with a $200.00 tip. Very cool.

Releasing me from my chains, they asked me to join them as a civilian in the snack bar. I told them I'd think about it while unloading the cart and that I'd see them inside. Marissa, one of the cart/snack bar girls and the photographer for this very book, was in the snack bar and had everything all cleaned up. The guys asked her if she would make a sandwich, and in the middle of trying to tell them she was closed up for the day, I told her in a low voice that this was a sandwich she *definitely* wanted to make. A California Club? Oh yes. For this she earned a $50.00 tip. She was floored. I had to go home and thanked the guys again for the fun. Marissa told me the next day that by the time she left, she had made 90 bucks. Not bad for ten minutes of labor in a snack bar.

What a blast. I wish I could be a private cart girl all the time! How awesome would that be if courses offered that for groups willing to pay the fee? Hey, now there's an idea whose time has really come!

Chapter Fifteen

Freaks, Geeks, and Cock-a-roaches

Yes, I know there is a glossary awaiting your inspection at the end of this book, but this chapter was so intriguing to me I just couldn't wait to give you a sneak preview with the following three terms that, once you read them, you'll see why they deserve their very own chapter:

Freaks: These are the total golf nuts. They golf four to seven days a week and sometimes thirty-six holes or more in one day. They are either *really* rich, *really* obsessed, or *really* running away from their lives — and other opportunities in life. I am not sure which of those choices they've chosen, and perhaps there are even more choices I'm not aware of yet, but their whole life is golf, golf and more golf. (Sound familiar?)

Geeks: One would think golf courses would be filled with Poindexter-ish, shy, quiet, quirky sort of folk. Well, surprise! There are very few of these guys actually here. Golf, no matter how slow-paced and un-athletic the game may seem, is an impossible sport that requires not only physical strength and accuracy, but also incredible mental patience. (See "temper tantrums" in the official glossary.) It is truly incredible to watch a real pro in action. They are soooo flipping good! Golfers are far from geeks, but it takes all types and so they are naturally included here.

Cock-a-roaches: EWWWWWW! These are the guys that take giant leaps over the line, and I am not talking about the line from their golf ball to the hole. Some of them steal from my cart, many say sicker things than I can even mention here, and a few even show you things you probably don't want to see — ever.

The Tee Time Girl Review

DAY: My first two weeks on the job
TITLE: A Serious Foursome
SET-UP: The 13th hole

You are in for a treat, as this is the adventure that prompted me to write this book. It happened one beautiful day as I was just getting used to the position of being the beverage cart girl, yet still learning the do's and don'ts on the fairways. I can't say this is a very funny review, but certainly one of my deepest secrets. It's a "hold on to your jaw so it doesn't land on the floor" tale. This story is a real shocker. A REAL SHOCKER!

The "cock-a-roach" in question was encountered at the bottom of the fourth hole for the first time. He was really quite good looking. He was well dressed, had a good body (hey, I can look), and damn if he wasn't a good golfer to boot. He appeared to be around 47 years old. Too old for me, but he was definitely to be complimented for keeping himself so well preserved — kind of like Kiefer Sutherland or Mel Gibson. In between there somewhere was this guy. It was clear that this group was playing serious money golf, for they halted me from a distance to shut down my cart for complete silence until they were through.

The entire group wanted only water at the tee box of hole five, so I figured this group may not be drinking, but they tipped me well enough, so I decided to pay close attention to them on the course. I knew I would see them on the eighth or ninth hole, and this time they were a little friendlier and had a few beers. They were still very serious, though.

The next time I saw them was on 13. These people must have brought some of their own booze because they were trashed, especially the cock-a-roach. On the tee box they all wanted shots. They asked me to follow them up the fairway as they wanted to have another shot and that they would pay for all the shots at that point and tip me. For behaving as messed up as he acted, the cock-a-roach hit the crud out of the ball from the tee box. Anyway, I followed them up to the fairway and two of them decided they didn't want any more to drink. After the cock-a-roach's friend hit, he decided he didn't want anymore to drink, either. His friends left with the carts to the green and the cock-a-roach was expected to walk up after hitting his ball. The cock-a-roach asked me to wait so he could pay for the drinks. Okay, sure, but I felt a little anxious because I really needed to get back to serving the rest of the golfers on the course.

After he hit, he asked for a ride and explained that he would "tighten me up" on what was owed me "plus my tip." Before I knew it, or could answer properly, he had jumped onto the cart. I was a little shocked, but I was new and figured, what the heck. I looked left to make sure no one was hitting up. When I looked back he stated, "Okay, here's your tip." This guy had pulled out his schvantz and had it lying on his leg and I swear, with no exaggeration, it was down to his knee. It was the biggest appendage any poor cart girl has probably *ever* been made witness to, before or since. Our best decisions are almost always made in hindsight. What follows are three possible ways the reality could have occurred — the male fantasy, my fantasy, and then the reality.

1 THE MALE FANTASY OF HOW THE
DIALOGUE AND ACTION WOULD ENSUE:

Me:

IS THAT THING REAL?

Him:

WHAT DO YOU THINK? DO YOU LIKE YOUR TIP?

Me:

*(Reaching to touch him and
not waiting for an answer)*

OH, *YES! MAY I?*

Him:

MMMMMMMM!

Me:

LET'S GO OFF BEHIND THOSE ROCKS.

*(We go off and have wild sex for
two minutes and I drop him off to his
friends with a freshly f***ed hairdo.)*

2 TWO: NOW, FOR MY FANTASY OF HOW
THE SCENARIO SHOULD HAVE HAPPENED:

Me:

IS THAT THING REAL?

Him:

WHAT DO YOU THINK? DO YOU LIKE YOUR TIP?

Me:

(*Pouting lip and batting eyelashes*)

YOU KNOW I WOULD LOVE TO TOUCH IT, BUT I HAVEN'T RECEIVED MY PAYMENT FOR THE DRINKS YET.

Him:

(*Opening his wallet*)

WILL $50 DO?

Me:

(*Gesturing to see the wallet*)

MAY I?

Him:

(*Handing me the wallet*)

Me:

(*Taking out all the money and throwing him his wallet back*)

THANKS!

Me:

(With a shrill scream and leaping out of the cart)

EEEEEEKKKKKKKK! HELP ME! PLEASE COME BACK
HERE AND GET YOUR FRIEND! OH MY GOD!

(Tears welling in my eyes.)

GET OUT!!!!!

*(Grabbing my cell phone and calling
the clubhouse, all the while screaming.)*

He gets out of the cart and runs to join his friends. I get in
my cart and drive away, never to return to them.

3 NOW, WHAT REALLY HAPPENED:

Me:

IS THAT THING REAL?

Him:

WHAT DO YOU THINK? DO YOU LIKE YOUR TIP?

Me:

TEMPTING, BUT . . . CASH IS MORE APPROPRIATE.
PERHAPS YOU COULD PUT THAT THING AWAY
NOW?

Him:

AH YES, QUITE RIGHT.

As we approached the green, he composed himself and gave what he owed for the drinks and, for me, a $10 tip. I wasn't quite sure what to say. I mean, this really freaked me out in so many ways. As I left, I kind of felt like $10 wasn't enough. Next time I'll choose option two, having worked out the whole hindsight and best-choice thing. Actually, there won't be a next time. I no longer give *anyone* a ride in the cart.

Now, get a grip, everyone still reading this book: hopefully you are a grown-up who purchased this book. Most people think, "How sad," or "That's too bad," or "What a creep." Yes, okay, all of the above, and then some, trust me, but it's not like I am twelve and this happened, and it's not too far out that it hasn't happened to a handful of other women in my position. I am also pretty sure that like Louie from the tournament chapter, he will wonder what the hell he did when he sobers up, and if ever out on my course again, will hope like hell I don't recognize him. For the cock-a-roach that's probably true, Louie can come back anytime!

I mean, who has never seen a porno flick or seen a dirty magazine? Come on, now. Be honest. It was creepy, but it was funny as hell, too, once all was said and done, so wipe that shocked look off of your face and continue reading the rest of the book.

Chapter Sixteen

Sluts, Strippers, and Sores

L et us get straight to the review:
I have heard of golf courses that have cabañas and tents set up where men can enjoy the paid pleasures of call girls posing as massage therapists. This is entirely illegal in California, of course, and the courses I have heard about were royally busted when caught. I have only heard stories. Men have offered a lot of money in hopes that I would flash them, but I, just like the super model Giselle, will never show nipple. (Or certainly never tell you if I did!) Now, I'm not a bad girl, but I see no harm in women who are. To each her own, I always say. I have seen men bring whores to the course to be their caddies. Hey, it's a career and from what I hear, a really old and profitable one. The golfers just tell the course that the girls are riders and most courses have a special fee for them. It's called a rider fee. On that particular day, I could think of many an implication to read into the word "rider."

I love variety and this kind of thing happens extremely seldom, but it's a great way to change things up for me. The drugs and sex, I can't get into with them, but I am not going to stop them or avoid them and not serve them. I don't mind watching a little, either, but I did have to turn away when one of the girls was giving a hummer to her guy. On one of my rounds by them, later, of course, after the "humming" was over, they even asked if I would do a "body shot" with the girls. I told them that drinking was not permissible while I was working, and that I couldn't even participate in the lime suck as I had a little cold sore (yuck), but that I would be happy to "direct," so to speak.

So the salt lick was to take place on a freshly spanked bottom. The boys liked that. The tequila shot was sucked out of

girl number two's cleavage. A little messy, but *very* effective. The spanked, salt-licked girl now held the lime in her teeth, which the tequila-shooting girl bit into with such tenderness I was almost breathless. The lime suck went on for a good two minutes. I can see what the appeal for you men must be in watching the girl-on-girl thing. It was really quite sexy, if I do say so myself. They all seemed quite happy to have performed their roles in my directing debut and, in the end, I was paid handsomely for the job!

Chapter Seventeen

Nature Boy

(A REALLY BAD POEM AND
I NEED IT IF I AM GOING TO HAVE
18 CHAPTERS IN THIS BOOK.)

Nature Boy

Nature Boy likes to take off his shoes.
Nature Boy likes to pee in the woods.
He waters the grass and the rocks and the tee box.
The world is his toilet, the golf course to frolic.

He smokes so much herb,
He can't remember his score.
I give him his candy,
He's got munchies, needs more.

He buys chips, and crackers, and beers, and cigars.
Cotton mouth not even Powerade could bar.

Nature Boy's lost and laughing his head off.
He aimlessly drives and cannot find his tee box.
He lights up another and again waters the rocks.
On his cell phone he tells all his friends he is sauced.

So golfers, beware searching for balls on the bank.
If it's yellow, you'll know, Nature Boy made it rank.

Chapter Eighteen

Temper Tantrums

won't claim I've saved the best for last, but you be the judge as we drive up to our last chapter together. Everyone has their moments of being roughly critical of themselves. No, no. This chapter is not about the guy who throws his putter across the dance floor because he drove all the way there only to three-jack the putt. And this is not for the person who yells out obscenities because he crushed the ball into the next fairway or into one of those notorious ball-eating bushes. This is for the *true* psychos out there.

This is the guy who breaks his putter in a tournament and then discovers he needs that club for the rest of the tournament and by rules of the game cannot borrow from anyone . . . well, duh!

You've probably heard about the guy who gets so mad he throws his clubs into the water, bag and all . . . *then* he has to go into the water to retrieve the bag because he left his keys in it. Well, the tantrum I witnessed was like this: This guy is walking off the green, blinded by his anger. He's cussing and swinging his putter and kicking the grass up. Making quite a mess of it, in point of fact. Meanwhile, his cart partner is in the bathroom and the others are ordering drinks from me. (Coincidence? I think not.) Anyway, he walks up to his clubs and starts pulling them out and bending the shafts on the side of the cart. I say to his friends, "Man, he must be really mad, he's breaking his clubs!" One of the guys drops the drink I just handed him and goes running up to him, screaming, "Stop, you fucker, those are MY clubs!" We all gasp.

You know, they have medication for people like this!

This, my friends, is the guy who silently walks from the hole, ball and putter in hand, face burning red, and has to sit in his cart, unable to move. Enter the cart girl, me, who unknowingly asks if he is all right. He looks up. Holy crud, the dude is CRYING! There's no crying in golf! It's freaking golf. How in the world can you cry over GOLF! Okay, I kind of stole that little bit, but it works here too and it's true.

This is the guy who is so wrapped up in how badly he's playing that he mistakenly drives his cart over a cliff and breaks his leg. He's so old that he has to be airlifted off the course. That's actually sad, really.

This is the guy who gets so mad at me because I refuse to serve him another Bloody Mary that he forfeits the game and complains to the head pro of my accusations that he is too drunk. Guess what, I still have my job! I should have taken his keys, too.

This is the guy who tees off to the left into the trees. He goes into the woods and hits his ball and manages to get the ball stuck in the branches. Thinking he can get the ball down by tossing his club skyward, he now has his ball and his club stuck up there. Now the dilemma: Does he find a better way or does he continue to chuck clubs up in the branches? I am a true believer that history has a way of repeating itself, and in this guy's case, the lesson was not learned the first time. Up went another club and stuck went that club. Now he's cussing and scratching his head and his partner is fed up waiting for him and leaves. Enter Cart Girl. I drive over, climb up on top of my cart and with a club in my hand rescue his other clubs and ball. Grown men can act like such babies!

There you have it, some of my experiences during the treacherous, yet exciting, journey through your golf course as your favorite — or not-so-favorite, you be the judge — beverage cart girl! I'll see you out there if you make it to my course and I will try my best to make you happy.

But buyers beware; you might just make it into book two!

Then again, you just might like that. . . .

Appendix

A Golf Thesaurus

(OF SORTS)

Listed below is a partial list of names, monikers, cutesy slang, etc., used to describe yours truly and all those of my kind. Now, keep in mind that these terms are most definitely *not* endorsed by the CGAOA (Cart Girls Association of America). But hey, they work for me:

Quench Wench

Beer Slut

Snatch Cart

Girlie

Snack Bitch

Beer Babe

HEY!

Nurse

Wet Nurse

My next ex-wife

Mother of my unborn children

Liquor Lassie

Her

And other variations of the position.

Glossary of Terms

For Errant or Not-So-Errant Golf Shots

Air-mailing the green: A shot hit well in direction and distance to the hole, but due to wind, or more precisely, *pilot error*, the ball travels off or over the green.

Ball hawking: The process of scavenging for golf balls on and around the course. Make sure you are only looking for balls that are out of bounds or out of play area. The biggest mistake of novice golfers is to pick up other people's balls while they're still "in play." Remember, as strange as it happens, some people accidentally hit their drive shot onto *other* fairways. I know that on my course people hit their balls from the 15th tee box onto the 17th fairway all the time. It is considered bad ball hawking manners if you, a player on 17, pick that ball up as a found lost ball.

Beating snakes: An exceedingly poor round of golf with little redeeming value, i.e., you might tell your wife or husband that you felt like you were "beating snakes" all day.

Break: In reference to putting, it is the curve due to the slope of a green.

Carry: The distance a golf ball must travel from impact (the moment the golf ball leaves the clubface) to the point where it first hits the ground. *Carry* is especially important when judging the distance to the green over a hazard (water, bunker, etc.).

Chili dip: Shots hit fat (as if the grass is the back of a human body and the arch the ball makes is the tummy), landing far short of target. Surprisingly, though, no large *turf burger* is dug up on this shot. Some people also call this a *chubby*.

(I think of a chubby as something entirely sick and perverted, however, much like myself.)

Choke: *v.* To collapse under a great deal of pressure, so that the muscles are incapable of performing to their greatest ability.

Chunk: *v.* Similar to a *chili dip*; the process of taking a large piece of turf before hitting the ball, resulting in a mis-hit that does not travel very far. *n.* A mis-hit of this type.

Crack: *adj.* Referring to a first-class or champion-caliber player. *v.* 1. To suffer a sudden collapse of good play, as in *choke*. 2. To hit a good drive.

Croquet-style: *adj.* A putting stance in which the player straddles the target line and faces the hole, swinging the putter like a croquet mallet.

Dance floor: *n.* The putting green.

Divot: A piece of turf removed with a golf shot. It is proper etiquette always to replace the divot, and to step the turf back in its original place. Many courses provide a container of sand in golf carts to fill your divots.

A Dog or a Rover: A ball that is hit really badly. A dog ball is a bad or less valuable ball that you don't mind losing. *Not* your Titleist Pro v 1 distance ball with the star symbol (✳✳✳) after it.

Dogleg: *n.* A hole or fairway characterized by a sharp turn in either direction, as in a *dogleg-left* or *dogleg-right* hole.

Drain: *v.* To sink a putt.

Duck hook: *n.* A violent hook (right-to-left) shot that normally travels low and hits the ground quickly.

Duff. *v.* To mis-hit a shot by hitting the ground before the ball.

Duffer: *n.* A bad golfer.

Explode: *v.* To escape from a sand bunker with a shot that displaces a large amount of sand along with the ball. Also called a *blast.*

Fatty Arbuckle: A shot hit so fat it exceeds the *chili dip* classification, but whose divot is too small to be granted full *turf burger* status.

Floater: *n.* 1. A shot struck from deep grass that comes out slowly and travels shorter than normal. Opposite of a *flyer.* 2. A variety of golf ball, rarely used, that floats in water.

Fried egg: *n.* A lie in which the ball is partially buried in the sand, sitting in its own hole. Also *plugged lie.*

A Gehrig or a Thurman Munson: A badly pulled putt, or short iron approach. (A DEAD YANK, read shank and you'll get yank, okay?)

Gimme: A short putt so close to the hole that your playing partners allow for you to simply pick it up — without taking the time to actually putt the ball into the hole. You'll hear, "That's a gimme!" during a casual and friendly round of golf, but it is not within the actual rules of golf. Don't forget, a *gimme* still counts as a stroke. It is just typically used as a time-saving and friendly gesture that is offered by your fellow playing competitors.

Going yard: This term can be used to describe a great drive. I, however, like to yell out "Going yard" when an opponent's shot goes out of bounds and ends up in somebody's backyard. When the homeowner, God forbid, is home and begins to scold you, look at them as though you have no idea what they are saying. Much like the look you receive from your gardener when he fails to show up for five weeks in a row. Suddenly, the person with whom you have had many a friendly conversation is unable to speak or comprehend any English. You can have a howling good time playing this game with the homeowner, if you can keep a straight face, that is. The lack of response causes most owners such frustration that they will quickly grow tired of the game. Scaring the be-Jesus out of the homeowner is one thing, in which case this game is acceptable, damaging their property is quite another. Karma will get you for walking away if you actually hurt someone or break something.

Gorse: *n.* A thick, prickly shrub usually found on links courses (especially in Great Britain) and apt to swallow errant golf shots.

Grip: The top part of the club held by the golfer, usually made from leather or rubber. Also, commonly used in reference to the manner in which the club itself is held. The two most common grips are the "Vardon" or overlapping grip (named after golfer Harry Vardon, in which the pinky finger of the bottom hand overlaps between the index and middle finger of the upper hand) and the "interlocking" grip, in which the index finger of the top hand is interlocked with the pinky finger of the bottom hand.

Hacker: *n.* An unskilled golfer, also duffer.

A Hoffa: A ball that is hit, and then surprisingly never seen or heard from again. Way out of bounds.

Hook: For the right-handed golfer, it is a golf shot that curves strongly from right to left. Moreover, for the right-handed golfer, this shot usually lands left of their target (the direction would be opposite for the left-handed golfer). Note: A lesser hooking action is commonly referred to as a "draw." A *draw* is a controlled right-to-left shot with a moderate curving action.

Jail: *n.* A spot from which it is almost impossible to play a safe shot.

Knee-knocker: *n.* A short putt, in the two- to four-foot range, that causes a golfer mental and physical anxiety.

Mulligan: The chance to replay your last shot — penalty free. Again, though common, a *mulligan* is not within the actual rules of golf.

Nice out: The term spoken by your opponent or friend when you have the perfect lie in the middle of the fairway and you hit a *Hoffa*.

A Phyllis, or a Diller: *Ugly* (even with all the plastic surgery) but with a successful result. (Mis-hit, or clubbed-clubbed fat shot, or thinned shot that ends with a great result.) Example: You hit the ball on the toe of your five-iron, but it caught the cart path, bounced high, and then rolled right up the guts of the fairway onto the green and was stopped by the pin.

Plumb bob: A method of aligning a putt or reading a green. You do this by facing the cup, raising the putter shaft to eye level, and looking at the hole with your dominant eye. For pros, I think this method is effective. For regular golfers, it just takes up golf time — and looks really funny.

Quail-high: *adj.* Describing a shot hit on a low, flat trajectory (after the way quails fly).

Quit: *v.* To give up on a shot while hitting it; to decelerate through the impact of a shot.

Rough: *n.* Long grass, usually found along the edges of the fairway.

Sandbagger: *n.* A golfer who lies about his playing ability in order to gain an advantage, particularly when betting.

Sand trap: *n.* A bunker; also referred to as a *trap*.

Scramble: A format in which all golfers hit the ball, starting at the tee (beginning of each golf hole). The ball in the best position is selected after each shot, and the process starts all over again, until the ball is putted/holed out. This format is good for beginners, as it alleviates the pressure of playing with better players.

Scrambler: *n.* A player who plays erratically, yet still scores well.

Scratch golfer: *n.* A player whose *handicap is* zero; one who receives no handicap strokes.

Shank: *v.* To hit the ball with the *housel* of the club, causing it to fly dramatically right and short. *n.* A shot of this type. The *shank* is typically considered the worst shot in golf — even worse than a *whiff.*

Sink: *v.* To hole out a putt.

Skins: *n.* A betting game in which the lowest score on a hole wins the wager for that hole; if any players tie, the bet carries over to the next hole.

Skull: *v.* To hit the ball above its equator with the leading edge of the club; to *top* the ball. *n.* A shot of this type.

Sky: *v.* To hit the ball extremely high. *n.* A shot of this type.

Slice: *v.* For right-handed players, to hit the ball sharply from left to right. *n.* A shot of this type. Unfortunately, this is the most common ball flight in golf.

Slicer: *n.* One who habitually slices the ball.

Snake: *n.* A very long putt, usually one that breaks several times.

Splash: *v.* To explode the ball from a sand bunker or deep rough. *n.* A shot of this type.

Stick: *n.* 1. The *flagstick.* 2. Slang for a golf club. *v.* To play a shot that finishes close to the hole.

Tailwind: *n.* A breeze that blows in the same direction as the shot, helping it fly farther.

Tee: *n.* 1. Typically, a wooden peg, on which the golf ball is placed for striking the ball at the beginning of any given golf hole. The *tee/teeing* ground is also referred to as the point from which the play of any given hole begins. *v.* To place the ball on a tee.

Tee box: *n.* Teeing ground.

Tee off. *v.* To play a tee shot.

Tight: *adj.* 1.Referring to a fairway or hole that is very narrow, usually lined on both sides by trees or hazards. 2. Referring to a lie when the ball is very close to the ground, with little grass beneath it. 3. Me, for cryin' out loud!

Toe: *n.* The end of the club head farthest from the shaft. *v.* To hit a shot with the toe of the club head. (I do this all the time.)

Triple bogey: *n.* A score of three over par on a hole.

Trouble: *n.* Rough, hazards, trees, other obstacles on a course, or *me.*

Turf burger: The gigantic divot taken (unnecessarily) by a lofted but badly mis-hit ball.

Vardon grip: *n.* See *grip.*

Visualization: *n.* The act of forming a mental picture of the correct swing or shot needed as a way to better prepare to make it happen.

Waggle: *v.* To move the club head and wrists in a flexing motion before swinging; used to relieve tension as part of a pre-shot routine. *n.* Any movement in this manner. It also makes your tush wiggle.

Whiff. *v.* To miss the ball completely with a swing. *n.* A shot that misses the ball completely; "air ball." A *whiff* is counted as a stroke — because the intent to hit the ball was there. On the other hand, a "practice swing" involves no intent to hit the ball.

Worm burner: *n.* A mis-hit shot that travels very low to the ground.

Yips: A slang word for missing many short putts — typically due to nerves or just simple uncertainty. Extreme nervousness over short putts that causes a player to miss the hole badly.

Zoysia: *n.* A warm-climate grass with coarse blades that can handle extreme temperature change. This is stretching it, sure, but hey, you've got to have a "z" in your glossary somewhere!